Safe, Loved AND Free

How hitting rock bottom
inspired my awakening and led me to the life
and love I'd always longed for

SITA

BALBOA.PRESS
A DIVISION OF HAY HOUSE

Balboa Press books may be ordered through booksellers or by contacting:

Balboa Press
A Division of Hay House
1663 Liberty Drive
Bloomington, IN 47403
www.balboapress.com
844-682-1282

Because of the dynamic nature of the Internet, any web addresses or links contained in this book may have changed since publication and may no longer be valid. The views expressed in this work are solely those of the author and do not necessarily reflect the views of the publisher, and the publisher hereby disclaims any responsibility for them.

The author of this book does not dispense medical advice or prescribe the use of any technique as a form of treatment for physical, emotional, or medical problems without the advice of a physician, either directly or indirectly. The intent of the author is only to offer information of a general nature to help you in your quest for emotional and spiritual well-being. In the event you use any of the information in this book for yourself, which is your constitutional right, the author and the publisher assume no responsibility for your actions.

Any people depicted in stock imagery provided by Getty Images are models,
and such images are being used for illustrative purposes only.
Certain stock imagery © Getty Images.

Scripture quotations marked KJV are from the Holy Bible, King James Version (Authorized Version). First published in 1611. Quoted from the KJV Classic Reference Bible, Copyright © 1983 by The Zondervan Corporation.

Print information available on the last page.

ISBN: 978-1-9822-7711-6 (sc)
ISBN: 978-1-9822-7712-3 (e)

Library of Congress Control Number: 2021923126

Balboa Press rev. date: 11/12/2021

Contents

Preface

It had been several years since I had been able to cry. You don't really notice while it's happening. Your heart just closes up, bit by bit, until you can't really feel anymore. That way, it doesn't hurt so much. If I'd had to feel it all back then, I wouldn't have made it through. So much pain. Going numb got me through that period. It was a long period. I was well practiced in hiding it all behind a smile, a joke. I was often the entertainer, the counselor to others. Funny how clearly we can see the way for others and yet remain blind to our own needs. More than I dared admit to myself, much less anyone else, I needed help. I was hoping someone would save me without my having to admit I needed saving.

I married him because he wanted to, and I didn't know how to say no. Does that sound crazy? I had never learned to discern what I wanted, always just pleasing others. *Don't disappoint anyone.* The guilt of saying no would've been unbearable. Besides, he played the part well. Prince Charming. Quite charming. Too charming.

I've since learned how charming narcissists can be.

And I suppose I was afraid. At twenty-eight, I saw him as my last hope at having a family of my own. Heartbreak in my past had brought me to the point that I didn't believe anymore that real love was part of the divine plan for me. So I wasn't head over heels … so what? He had a good job and seemed like the family type. Maybe it was time for me to lower my romantic expectations and just settle.

Of course I told myself that I loved him. I could always get caught up in feeling in love. Conveniently, you don't have to really see the person you want to be in love with. You can pretend he's someone else, in your mind. Just see the stuff that feeds the image you want him to have and ignore the rest. Reality is overrated.

Unconsciously, I had made the decision to ignore the cries of my heart and let my head steer the ship. Well, I kind of knew, but I didn't want to see it. After all the pain and disappointment of following my heart, I was too exhausted for anything else. The rest of the world seemed to commend being practical. Maybe my idealistic youth was over, and it was time to think practically. Oh, ego, how very clever you are at making the wrong choices seem right!

Five years passed so quickly. Here I stood, baby in my arms. None of it had been the way I'd dreamt as a girl—not the wedding, not the pregnancy or childbirth, not any of it. Pretending we were like any other couple was wearing me out. My Prince Charming dropped his act once he figured he had me. It happened gradually, but the arrival of our son seemed to be the final guarantee in his mind. Now he didn't have to pretend anymore. I was stuck in a marriage with no intimacy, no joy, no trust. I felt like I was just part of the facade he needed to present his perfect self to the world. He needed me to fill that role, but behind closed doors, it was just about power. Parenting had become yet another area he felt he needed to one-up me in, instead of the shared joy it could've been. I felt isolated, depressed, and empty.

When I told him I was feeling depressed and lonely, he got angry with me for not trying harder to find friends. Back in Germany, I had lots of good friends, but he'd taken me away from them by getting himself transferred to France. He never liked them anyway. He wanted me to himself, but he didn't care if I was happy or not.

Is this the kind of mother I want to be? I thought. Depressed and emotionally exhausted, like my own mother. I sensed that I would end like her if I didn't get out now. Intuitively, I knew that I would pass this legacy of emptiness on to this sweet, innocent bundle of love in my arms if I stayed. Have you ever felt like your soul was dying?

But how could I leave? I was in a foreign country with no job, no family, and a nine-month-old baby. How would we survive? I had no idea. All I knew was that I couldn't stay because I couldn't breathe anymore. Sometimes the only way out is to take a leap of faith. My love for my son gave me the courage. "I will not pass this down to you, my sweet, innocent child. I will do whatever it takes to give you a life filled with love and happiness."

Generation after generation, we hand down our unresolved issues. Intuitively, at the time, I knew this. Today, I know it's called intergenerational trauma. Pain, anger, guilt—they don't just go away when our ancestors pass on. They are energy, and energy never dies. But it can be transformed; it can be healed. Somehow I knew this at the time. I sensed my mother's presence telling me to break free, like she wished she had. "Don't repeat my life," she said. She had been depressed and lonely and eventually became very ill. I was well on my way to following in her footsteps. But I refused to hand this burden down to my beautiful boy. *If I don't do the work, he will have to.* I made the decision to break the cycle.

I realized that the greatest gift I could give my child was to be a happy mom, so I set about becoming one. This book is my offering to those of you who want to do the same. Happiness is our birthright, and it is possible for each of us to find it. Twenty years later, my son and I live magical and blessed lives. He's happy, successful, and a joy to be around. We've shared many adventures, much laughter, and some hard times as well, but we have come through it all and have been able to create the lives of abundance and joy that we deserve.

No matter what you've been through, how exhausted, empty, or hopeless you may feel, or how bleak things look at the moment, change is possible—and it can begin right now. Even if you see no way out, trust that there is one. Meditation and understanding the law of attraction helped me to heal and release my past as well as create a magical and amazing new life.

There is no difference between you and me. I found a way to change my life that works, and it can work for you as well. If I can do this, so can you. As I've often told my clients, it's not easy, but it's worth it! I want to help you to live a better life. Are you ready to shift from fear to love?

The Cheese Sandwich

Imagine that you had a cheese sandwich, but you weren't ready to eat it. Maybe you felt that eating it right away might upset your stomach, or you just didn't feel like eating it yet, so you decided to put it in a drawer for later. But perhaps deep down, you didn't really even want to eat it later; you didn't really like cheese sandwiches, so you easily forgot it was there. You let yourself get so busy and distracted by other things, people, work, and more that you simply forgot you'd ever had this sandwich.

Time passed, and the sandwich started to go bad. At first you could ignore the smell, but eventually it got so strong that you had to notice it. You followed the smell to the drawer, but you felt very hesitant to open the drawer. You had a vague memory that the thing you put in that drawer was something you didn't want. You couldn't remember exactly what it was or why you didn't want it, and this uncertainty made you a little afraid.

What if I open the drawer and the smell gets so bad that I pass out or die? What if I can't handle it?

But the smell began to affect not only your health but also your relationships. People coming to your home noticed it and didn't want to visit you anymore. They didn't say it was because of the smell, but you knew. Somehow you knew that the only way to get your life back was to get rid of the awful smell. And the only way to do that was to open the drawer.

So, you opened it, and it was *awful*! The smell got ten times stronger, and you thought you were going to be sick! Your eyes started to water, and you gagged when you looked at it. For a brief moment, you wished you'd never opened the drawer.

Then you had an idea. You put on some gloves and lifted the remains of the sandwich out of the drawer. You threw it in the garbage and put it all outside on the curb, to be picked up and gone forever. Then you went back with some cleanser and a cloth and scrubbed the drawer clean. You threw away the cloth and the gloves and left the drawer open to air dry.

It was one of the hardest things you'd ever had to do, and you felt pretty exhausted. After a restful, deep sleep, you woke up and noticed that your room smelled really good. You no longer had to avoid looking at the drawer. You felt lighter and free to move around and take deep breaths again.

You realized that there might be other drawers like this one in your future, but now you knew what you had to do to clean them out, so it wasn't as scary anymore. Empowered and liberated, you knew you could handle whatever else you had hidden away.

This is how the process of clearing out our suppressed emotions and memories works. This is why we do it. Sure, we could just keep spraying air freshener to cover the smell, but we all know that doesn't solve the problem.

Introduction

*Your task is not to seek for love but merely to seek and find
the barriers within yourself that you have built against it.*
—Rumi

I came upon the ideas in the law of attraction several years before hearing the term. It was my meditations and reading about the yogic teachings of the chakra system, as well as Buddhist principles, which introduced me to the idea that it is our internal lives that create our external ones. I learned firsthand that by transforming fear into trust as a meditation exercise, I could not only feel stronger and more confident about my life, but I could even open myself to experiences that helped reduce those fears.

For example, in the first year after my overseas move back to Winnipeg (after seventeen years in Europe), alone with my six-year-old son and a rapidly dwindling savings account to live on, I was in a situation that would have normally caused much fear or even panic. Several job prospects presented themselves, but none worked out for longer than a month or two. In this way, I managed to keep paying my bills while continuing my inner search for whatever my true calling was.

I meditated every morning for thirty minutes to an hour on my root chakra (at the base of the spine) and found that, in addition to turning my fear into a calm assurance that all would be well with us, there were also manifestations in the material world that strengthened that conviction. Unexpected checks would arrive in the mail, and this, along with the short-term jobs, enabled me to keep going from month to month. There were no long-term guarantees, but as time passed and these events continued, my faith in my ability to cocreate my life grew.

Through much soul searching in that period, I found myself eventually leading meditation groups, in which I felt particularly called to introduce this way of life to others.

In our Western world, you can imagine how well it went over when I told people that the best way to approach their problems was to sit and meditate on them! Not many were receptive; the idea sounded far too out there for a society of practical, rational, and rather controlling thinkers.

And then came the book *The Secret*, which was strongly marketed and quickly became very popular. It made my work easier now that people were more familiar with the concept, but I found the book and the DVD to be an oversimplified version of these ancient truths. I was concerned that people would try it out the way it was presented, and after either no success or a short-lived one, they would decide it doesn't work.

In order to allow more good into our lives, it is necessary to remove the hidden blocks we are carrying. There are negative beliefs that you are not aware of, and they have cocreated the life you are living now. Creating a new life involves more than just attracting more positive. It's more than just making lists and vision boards of what you want to have. It means becoming aware of and releasing all the negative beliefs you have that are blocking you from manifesting these desires.

The way the book presented it, I feared that many people would buy into it for the purpose of getting rich, which meant, in my opinion, that they would not have understood the most basic principle behind it: *there is such abundance in the Universe that there is no need for us to hoard.*

If people were approaching the law of attraction from this fear-of-scarcity need to hoard, I knew it would not work for them. Perhaps they would succeed in some initial attempts at attracting more wealth, but over the long term, they would come up against a brick wall. We have to replace our need to amass wealth with a faith that we will "receive each day our daily bread." Without faith that the Universe will continue to provide for us, fear eventually takes over again, and people find themselves unable to receive all the good things they desire.

Because it was so close to my heart to help people attain a deeper and more reverent understanding of this powerful truth, I decided to offer a class, based entirely on the law of attraction. In fact, I was told to do so during meditation, despite my misgivings about *The Secret*.

I think of it more as allowing than attracting, because I believe that the benevolent Universe wants us to be happy, prosperous, healthy, and loved. We don't need to attract that as much as we need to simply open the doors that we've shut along the way. I focused more on helping people remove the beliefs they were unconsciously carrying that were blocking them from receiving all that the Universe wanted them to have. I taught that the Universe (Creator, Source, or whatever name you want to use) is loving and absolutely capable of manifesting all of our desires and more. But rather than needing to *attract* all that we need, we could become aware that we are constantly surrounded by bountiful blessings. All we need to do is open ourselves to receiving them.

For years, I have watched every single person who participated in my class change their lives for the better. I have admired the courage they found to do the deep and often difficult inner work that is necessary. It was easy to see who would experience more subtle change and whose lives would change more profoundly. What they put in was what they got out of it. Digging up beliefs that had been blocking them all their lives sometimes felt worse before things got better. Bringing self-critical beliefs into our conscious minds can be a painful process. As long as they remain hidden, we don't have to face our self-rejecting thoughts. But those who were willing to do this work always experienced changes like better health, better relationships, more job satisfaction, and a general increase in happiness. More than anything, this approach to life gave them a sense of empowerment over their lives, as it had for me years before.

As a species, I see that we are moving toward a higher awareness about our existence on this planet. I have noticed that along with me, there are others teaching these principles in little pockets all over the Western world. People are more open and receptive than they have been in the past because, quite frankly, they are noticing that the way we've lived in the past few centuries has left us unfulfilled, to say the least.

We continue to experience wars, even though we understand on one level that violence only begets more violence. Our politicians disappoint us with their corruption, greed, and scandals. Families have fallen apart, and our youth have never been in so much danger of choosing a self-destructive path. Our health care systems are run by megapharmaceutical giants, and people are getting sicker and sicker. Depression is on the rise, as are anxiety and obesity. We hardly know what is in the food we are eating, as we have become so far removed from its source. Half the world is dying from not having enough to eat and the other half from having too much. We have become addicted to consuming, which affects not only our bodies but also our bank accounts.

Our school systems leave children with an overdeveloped intellect yet almost no practice in compassion, empathy, or how to have healthy relationships. We have been taught that it's every person for themselves; there's not enough to go around, so do whatever you have to do to get your share of the pie before someone else takes it. In the world of business, cruel and inhumane practices toward other human beings are considered acceptable and even clever.

And all of this is based on the absolutely mistaken idea that the loving Source that created us is not able or willing to supply us with all that we need in order to not only survive but actually enjoy our lives!

To me, it sounds like it's time for a change. And change is coming. Each of us in our little group or on our own needs to do what we can to raise our awareness and become free from this mentality of scarcity. Only then will we be able to truly be happy for our neighbour's success without fearing that there won't be enough left for us as well. Only then will we be able to put the needs of those less materially fortunate above our own fearful need to hoard more for ourselves. Only when we truly understand that we each have the ability to create the life we desire, completely independent of what those around us are achieving or not achieving, will we cease to see the other as a threat. All that you want your life to be is possible. Everything you imagine can and will come true. Follow the exercises I've laid out for you in this book to raise your awareness of what is blocking you, and do the meditations, tapping, and journaling regularly. Then sit back and watch your life unfold in miraculous ways.

What is the law of attraction?

It's quite simple really. Like attracts like, and everything is energy. Thoughts, feelings, even your physical body—they are all forms of energy. Send out positive thoughts and receive positive energy in return. Well, if it's that simple, why isn't everyone using it, and why isn't it working for everyone?

Not Just Positive Thinking

A lot of people have an oversimplified idea of the law of attraction. It can seem in the early stages of learning about this powerful law that it is nothing more than the power of positive thinking. While observing our thoughts and learning to filter out the negative is an important part of the law of attraction, it can actually be detrimental to stop there in our search.

When we are processing suppressed pain, for example, it is very important to allow space for that pain in the present moment. The same applies for suppressed fear, anger, or any other feeling. These feelings strongly affect the energy we are sending out as long as they stay suppressed; it is crucial work in clearing our energy that we express them in some way.

Sometimes, people with a limited understanding of the law of attraction will cut off a person who is finally acknowledging pain that she was in denial of for twenty years, by saying, "Stop being negative! Focus on the positive!"

This is not helpful!

Of course, we don't want to encourage anyone to wallow in lower-vibrational emotions for too long, but it is very important that we offer them empathy as they are finding their voice. Compassionate listening doesn't mean you allow someone to gossip or dump their emotional garbage on you time after time. It means recognizing when a person needs to speak their truth on a subject that they have been afraid to speak about before and giving them the gift of your loving attention. There is much healing to be found in this. Feeling heard is more powerful in helping someone you care about on their healing journey than any advice you could offer.

If you notice after a few weeks that the person is beginning to spiral downward (and pull you with them), gently and lovingly redirect the conversation, but make sure they have felt heard before doing this.

For example, "Wow, I never realized how difficult that time in your life was. I wish I could've been there to help. But I'm here now. How about you and I go for a silent walk in the woods together? I find nature healing."

One of the major blocks to get past when encountering these principles for the first time is the feeling that it is about blame. It is an unpopular idea for some people that their thoughts created the life they are now living. I have often had people who are suffering in one form or another ask me accusingly, "Are you saying that this is all my fault?"

And the answer to that is a great big "No!" This path is about empowerment, not blame. Of course, your thoughts have influenced your life up until now, but the most powerful thoughts we have are those that we are not even conscious of. How can you be blamed for thoughts that are hiding in your subconscious mind? You can't. So let go of the idea of blame and open your mind to the incredible empowerment that will come as you become more aware of those thoughts (or subconscious beliefs) and learn how to change them.

Taking responsibility for creating the life you are living is not the same as taking the blame. It's not about making you feel guilty—God knows we don't need any more of that. We have ideas—mostly false ones—that we created, usually at a very young age. They are sending out energy that causes experiences to manifest for us that correspond to those ideas.

For example, you overheard your father saying that he hated his job, but he had to do it to keep food on the table. He wished he could be a carefree kid again. At the tender age of six years old, you decided that life as an adult was hard, and work was not something you enjoyed, but you had to do it; otherwise, you would go hungry. So, you enter adulthood with these messages playing like recordings in your head. The problem is they've been playing so long you don't even notice them anymore! But they are steering the ship nonetheless.

You will never find your dream job as long as this belief is steering you—and believe me, it is. You will always feel like life is hard, others seem to have it easier, and you don't understand why. It's because that's what you believe in. Your thoughts have become your reality.

So, what are you going to do? Blame the six-year-old who created this limiting belief and feel guilty for wasting so many years in unfulfilling jobs? Or are you going to learn how to access that belief in your subconscious mind, change it, and find the job of your dreams? The first is debilitating; the second is empowering. The choice is yours. You can live in regret and anger for the rest of your life, or you can harness the power of the present moment and create a new life from here on.

Until we do this work, we will continue to sabotage ourselves and our lives with these hidden thoughts. Some have tried to apply the principles of the law of attraction to their lives without understanding this and have falsely concluded that it does not work.

Nothing could be further from the truth. The law of attraction is real and very, very powerful. Your ego would like you to believe it doesn't work. That way, you can stay trapped in your old ways, and your ego will stay in control of your life (more on this in chapter 2). All through this book (and beyond), you will be confronted with your ego in the form of fears, excuses, rationalizations, distractions, and judgments.

To overcome ego and its many clever disguises, I suggest meditation.

What Is Meditation?

> In the attitude of silence the soul finds the path in a clearer light, and what is elusive and deceptive resolves itself into crystal clearness. Our life is a long and arduous quest after Truth. (Mahatma Gandhi)

Meditation is also quite simple, in theory. To meditate is to bring your awareness to the present moment, letting go of past and future. To do this, you simply focus your attention on your breathing. Don't try to rid your mind of thoughts or to chase them away when they arise. This will only frustrate you.

Instead, let them be there, but keep your attention on your breathing. Breathe as if it were not an involuntary instinct but instead as if you had to make each breath happen through your intention. You might try saying in your mind as you breathe, "I am breathing in now; I am breathing out now."

You can also use the simple technique of counting your breaths. I like to count to four as I'm breathing in and then to eight as I'm breathing out. That way, I stay focused on the breathing, and I ensure that I empty out all the stale air from my lungs. This helps the next in breath to go deeper, which is very relaxing and healing. Be aware of the natural pause between your in and out breaths. Just notice it.

As you do this, your level of awareness shifts from a state of ego to a state of soul. You will recognize this by a feeling of deep peace and calm. When you are in this state, you can see through the tactics (mentioned above) that ego uses to stop you from having the life you deserve.

When you are in this state, you can access those hidden thoughts in your subconscious mind and change them. When you are in this state, you are so directly connected with the creative impulses of the Universe that your power to cocreate your life is much stronger than it would be in your normal waking state.

When you meditate regularly, you naturally live more and more in this higher state of awareness, and in terms of the law of attraction, this means *being in the flow*.

What Is Visualization?

> Imagination is everything. It is the preview of life's coming attractions. (Albert Einstein)

Visualization is a powerful tool in cocreating your life. It is very similar to meditation, but it includes your imagination. If you can imagine it, you can manifest it. If you have limited thinking that tells you it's impossible, or that you can have it only if you work hard, then it will not show up in your life (unless you work hard). But it doesn't have to be that way.

Your thoughts become your reality. It is in the mind, not the external world, that you are most effective in creating the life you want. You begin just as with any other meditation—focusing on your breath. After a few minutes, you can begin to imagine a certain situation that you desire to manifest in your life. Visualize as much detail as possible, so that it seems real. Let yourself feel what it feels like to have already manifested it.

Some people have trouble seeing things in their meditations, so they worry that they won't be able to manifest anything. The more powerful part of the visualization is creating in yourself the feeling of already having the situation or thing you want to manifest. The feeling is the energy you send out, which in turn attracts the thing you desire. You don't necessarily have to see it to do this. Visualization is just a tool to help you get to the feeling.

There are two possible outcomes of doing a visualization:

1. It lifts your vibrations so that they match the frequency of that which you desire. Since like attracts like, lifting your energy is like clearing the pathway and opening the door to let your desires in.

2. If there is a block to receiving this into your life, when you try to visualize or feel like you have it, the block will come up. Becoming aware of it will give you the opportunity to work on removing it, so noticing any resistance in your visualization is a good thing.

What Is Emotional Freedom Technique?

Put away your skepticism, this really works … I have … had great results with tapping in my own life. (Wayne Dyer)

EFT is a method of healing by tapping your fingers lightly on acupressure points while making statements about your feelings, beliefs, or experiences in order to release blocks in your flow of energy. It was developed by Gary Craig. His website, www.emofree.com, explains everything you need to know about it.

I have found it to be an incredibly powerful tool in transforming feelings, changing unhealthy beliefs, and even healing physical symptoms.

For more resources on meditation, visualizations, and EFT, please go to my website: www.iamsita.com.

Attracting Money

One of the things I noticed friends doing after reading *The Secret* was writing themselves checks for $100,000 (or whatever amount) and putting them up on their ceiling or bulletin board. This is supposed to help them feel that the money is coming. The problem I see here is that if you are doing this—or any other activity—with the goal of attracting money into your life, then you are coming from a place where you don't believe that you have enough money. If you don't believe you have enough, you are in a mental state of lack. If you feel lack, you are doubting that the Universe is abundant. If you doubt that the Universe is abundant, how can you truly believe that there is enough for you?

I propose that we begin by feeling that we are already wealthy. It doesn't matter how much or how little you have in your bank or wallet. Stop saying you can't afford this or that and instead say, "I have money, and I choose not to spend it on this."

Tell yourself that you are already wealthy. Meditate and visualize yourself wealthy so that you can really feel it. When you feel that you are already living in abundance, then you believe that there is abundance in the Universe. When you believe that the Universe is abundant—when you truly believe that and do the work to unblock yourself from receiving—abundance will and must come to you.

You don't have to try to attract the money you want into your life. Just allow it. Believe it's there and keep your vibrations high. Unclog your pipes and let it flow. It's much easier than you think. Stop trying and start allowing. Relax, breathe, and believe.

WHAT DO YOU REALLY WANT?

You can't get what you want, till you know what you want.
—Joe Jackson

Let's start by getting clear on what we actually want. We are often so bombarded with marketing ads and societal pressures that tell us what we should want that it can be difficult to weed through it all. Many of us find ourselves unconsciously striving toward the attainment of material goals or romantic partnerships without a clear idea of what we are really looking for or why. No wonder so many of us feel unfulfilled despite "having it all." You've got the big house, the new car, you take a yearly big holiday somewhere in the sun … yet when you look in the mirror every morning you feel like something's missing. Having what everyone else has, or is telling you, you should want, will never fulfill you. The Universe knows what you truly desire and is more than willing to give it to you, but as long as you are asking for other things, you are not open to this. Getting in tune with your true desires is the first step toward having them manifest.

Exercise

Please do one step at a time without reading ahead.

Part 1

Take a few minutes to answer the following questions in writing:

- What do you want?
- Why are you reading this book?
- What changes would you like to see in your life?

Part 2

Now review what you have written. Ask yourself, "What is behind the thing(s) that I desire?"

For example, if you wrote "wealth," what is it that you imagine wealth will give you?

If you wrote "a new job," what do you believe that will bring?

If you wrote "to find my soul mate," what feeling would that give you?

Do you think more money will bring you a feeling of security? Fewer worries? A more harmonious marriage?

Do you believe a new job will bring you more happiness? A sense of purpose? Respect?

Are you hoping that finding your soul mate will end your loneliness? Fill the void in your heart? Prove to yourself and the world that you are worthy of love?

Part 3

Write these things down and ask yourself again, "What is behind my desire for a harmonious marriage? My sense of loneliness? The void in my heart?" And so on. Keep asking until you get to the root of your desires. When you end up with a simple word like "peace," "love," or "freedom," you can stop there.

Now make a conscious decision to *focus on this root desire and to let go of all of your ideas on how to get there.* Resist the temptation to start planning out how you are going to achieve this goal and learn to leave it up to the Universe. All that you thought you wanted was *your idea* of how to get to your deepest desire. But very often, our own ideas of how to get there are false. When we are planning the way, our egos inevitably get in the way and lead us down false paths; that is to say, paths that seem to offer what we are longing for but in the end leave us either unsatisfied or, worse yet, with the opposite outcome!

For example, you might be wishing for a feeling of peace and be convinced that paying off your debts will give you this. So you think it's money that you need, and you play the lottery. Let's suppose that you actually win—enough to pay off all your debts and still have some leftover to live a comfortable life. Studies have shown that immediately following a big win like this, people do tend to experience a high, but it is short-lived, and in many cases, people find themselves more miserable than they were before winning the money. Why is that?

We all have a yearning inside of us for something undefinable. In Western society, beginning in our school years or earlier, we are trained to seek material success in our lives rather than spiritual fulfillment. So, most of us, unless we receive spiritual education elsewhere, are left in the dark as to how that yearning could be satisfied. Naturally, we seek to fulfill it in ways that we are taught, so we convince ourselves that more money, success, fame, prestige, or possessions will do the trick.

And here's the rub: Imagine getting all of those things only to realize one quiet evening, while sitting all by yourself at your giant swimming pool and gazing up at the stars, that the emptiness inside you is still there. All that you thought you needed to fill it you now have, yet it's still there. But now you have no more ideas. You could strive for even more money, even more possessions, but eventually you would have to admit that the void inside you is just getting bigger. Your way—the way of your ego—is not working.

The Universe is far better equipped to lead us to the fulfillment of our desires than we are. We do not possess the view of the bigger picture, which is why we often end up on the wrong road. Sometimes tragically, we are offered the road to fulfillment and turn away from it, because our limited view prevents us from seeing where it will lead us. Perhaps you dream of opening your own business but turn down a job that would offer you the very skills and experience you would need to do so. Or you are searching for your soul mate and spending so much of your time on internet dating and going to the gym that you turn down the opportunity to help out at a volunteer event in your local church that happens to be run by the very person the Universe is trying to connect you with!

This is why it is more important to learn to connect with your inner voice on a regular basis and follow it throughout your day. You don't have to come up with a plan for your happiness. If you are in touch with your Source, you will receive guidance that may not make any sense at all in terms of achieving your desires. But you need to follow it anyway. So, there is a place for planning and doing; however, it comes after the inspiration or guidance from Source, not in place of it.

You will likely never see more than what the next step is, and it is important that you take it anyway. Gandhi freed an entire country from colonial oppression with this approach. "One step enough for me," was a line in his favorite Christian hymn. In his autobiography, he shared that he never made a decision without meditating on it first, even if it took days to gain the clarity he needed.

Our imaginations are limited, but "with God, all things are possible" (Matthew 19:26). By trying to be in control of the how, you are likely blocking yourself from ever getting to where you want to be. Learn to follow instead of trying to lead all the time. Focus on your desire, send out the intention during meditation, and then let go and leave the rest to Source.

Exercise

Letting go of this feeling of control is, of course, difficult. Try this visualization to help you: Take a deep breath or two, close your eyes, and imagine that you are standing in front of a house. See the details of the house: how big, what color, how many windows, old or new?

Now see yourself walking into the house. Notice how you feel. Nervous? Excited? Calm?

Look around and see the furniture in the different rooms. Now you see a staircase, leading downstairs.

You take the staircase. Do you go down the stairs slowly or quickly? What feeling do you have as you descend? The basement is dark. How does that feel?

You see in the far corner a glimmer of light. As you walk toward it, you see that it is a mirror, reflecting a little beam of light coming in from a small window.

Now you are standing in front of the mirror. Take a deep breath, look directly into it, and notice who you see. It may be a version of yourself that you've never seen before, or an image of yourself as a child. It can be anything at all. What is the feeling that comes to you from this image? Let yourself feel that you can trust this reflection of your inner wisdom, no matter how it presents itself to you.

Now, ask this part of yourself, "What do I want?" And just breathe as you receive your answer. It may come in words, images, or feelings. Accept whatever comes to you. Take a few moments to just sit, listen, and breathe.

When you feel ready, you can thank the image for its guidance and walk back up the stairs and out of the house. Look back at the house one last time before you open your eyes.

Immediately after you are finished with this visualization, record your insights and compare them with what you wrote at the beginning of this chapter.

My Story

I wasn't used to knowing what I wanted. I'd been told what I should or shouldn't want all my life. I had been trained to focus on the needs of others—not my own. So when Kurt came along and told me he was going to marry me, I went along. I don't think I ever asked myself if I wanted it too. It wasn't something that had ever mattered.

Looking back, I see signs that told me it would not make me happy to marry him, but I ignored them. I was thirty years old, and society told me that I needed to get married and have kids, or else I'd be some kind of misfit.

Our wedding day was a nightmare. I'd bought myself a dress in a department store on my own, because there was no one around to help me shop. The only dress I felt comfortable in, of all that I tried on, happened to be black. I wore some old shoes I had—nothing fancy. The least I thought I could do to make myself look beautiful on what was supposed to be my special day was to style my long, black hair nicely.

Kurt and I stood in the bathroom mirror at my father's home as I started working with my hair. He looked over at me, almost in disgust, and said, "You're not going to make your hair all big and curly, are you?"

Big and curly was exactly what I was going for, but now that he'd expressed his distaste for it, I quickly said, "No, of course not." I felt ashamed for having intended to do it that way. I had no hair or manicure appointments. I was doing it all myself. Truth be told, I didn't even know that most brides get these things done for them. My mother had been deceased for eleven years by then, and no one else stepped in to help me out.

I didn't question that. I was used to it not being about me. I took a scrunchie and pulled my hair back into a ponytail, then halfway through again so it hung there in a loop. It was the way I usually had my hair if I was doing housework or cooking. Kurt looked at me and nodded his approval.

Did he not want me to look beautiful on our wedding day? Or was it another random act of control, just to see if I'd do what he wanted?

It didn't stop with him. My father had invited people I barely knew to our wedding, even though I'd specifically said that I wanted it to be family only. That wasn't true either. Kurt wanted it to be small, and I once again pretended that I wanted that too. Deep inside, I was longing for that dream wedding, where the church was filled with people who gazed at me in awe as I glided down the aisle, but I didn't dare admit that to Kurt. He'd have laughed in my face.

My father had asked a friend to make us a wedding cake, which upset Kurt because he thought it was tacky. I told my father I didn't want it, which made him angry. I was stuck between these two men who wanted different things, trying to please them both. No one, not even I, seemed to care about what I wanted! I was completely out of touch with myself, with my own needs and desires. This was most evident on the day of a special event like this, but it was the common thread that ran through my whole life.

My wedding day, like my life, was about everyone else but me. No wonder.

As the song goes, "You can't get what you want till you know what you want." Nothing can manifest unless it can first be imagined. I couldn't even imagine what it must be like to feel special. I couldn't imagine being the center of attention. I couldn't imagine having a partner who would put my needs before his. And that was the problem.

When we're stuck in a pattern, it can be very hard to imagine life without it. To experience any of the things I just mentioned would have pushed me out of my comfort zone. There was a familiar feeling, a kind of false safety, in staying stuck where I was. I obviously wasn't ready to leave the role of the ever unappreciated and overlooked girl.

All I wanted was to make Kurt happy, to avoid having him get upset with me for anything. Perhaps somewhere deep inside, by marrying him, I was hoping to prove to myself and to the world that I was worthy of love after all. Then no one could point their finger and say, "Something must be wrong with her. She's not married."

I needed their approval. I needed his approval. I thought having that would make me happy. I wanted to feel safe and secure. I wanted to belong. I wanted to feel like I'd found my place in the world. I thought if I married him—despite all the warning signs—I'd find all that. I was wrong.

ASKING

Ask for what you want and be prepared to get it.
—Maya Angelou

How good are you at asking for what you need? It may sound simple, but for most of us, it is not. Unless you had the ideal experience of receiving everything you needed every time you needed it as a child, you probably have learned that asking can be a risky endeavor. If what you asked for was denied often enough, you've probably learned to pretend you don't need it.

Maybe you asked your parents to spend more time with you, and they were always busy with other things. So you stopped asking. It didn't mean you were content to play alone. You felt lonely, but the disappointment every time you asked just made that feeling worse, so you told yourself you were OK. You lied to yourself so that you didn't have to face how hurt you were. You might even have told yourself that you preferred to play alone. This is a defense reaction of the human psyche, which helps protect us from falling into utter despair at times like these. It serves us well as children, in situations where we are helpless to change, but it can lead to creating blocks that get in our way later on.

As an adult, you may be unable to receive the companionship of others because you've convinced yourself of the lie that you don't need them. You have a hard time finding friends because you've internalized the belief that you don't need any. You had to tell yourself that lie to survive the lack of attention in your childhood, and now that lie stops you every time you come close to having an experience of companionship. *If no one had time for me in the past, it must mean that I don't matter. Why would anyone want to be friends with someone who doesn't matter?*

You wouldn't dare ask it of anyone. How can you ask for something that will just be denied you again? It would hurt too much. The feeling of lack is still there, but you have convinced yourself that you don't want friends. In reality, you don't know what you want. All you know is that there is something missing—a need that is not being fulfilled.

The first step in asking for what we need is admitting to ourselves that we need it. Meditation is a great help here, as it bypasses the limits of our conscious mind and sheds light on the things we have suppressed. It can be a painful process to realize some of the needs we had to put on the back burner for so many years—often basic human needs like being loved for who we are or getting a hug when we need one. But as adults, it is necessary to finally cry those unshed tears of our childhood in order to move forward into the lives we want to have. The crying is a sign that you're admitting to yourself that you needed that loving attention after all. They are the tears that would've been too painful to cry when you were little and helpless, but today they are a vital part of your healing process.

The second step, now that you've acknowledged what you need, is to be able to ask for it. Just because you now know that you need to feel like you are important to someone, and you need them to show you that by spending more time with you, doesn't mean you won't still feel some fear about asking for it. Or maybe as a child you had too much responsibility, so today you feel like no one helps you with all of your work or appreciates all that you do. Now you've uncovered the false belief that created that situation: *I'm alone in this world. No one cares about me. Everyone else's needs matter more than mine.* What now? Can you ask for help?

It will be scary at first, but if you've done the necessary inner work, you won't be disappointed. The first thing you need to do is to change that false belief. Be careful that you are asking with an open heart and not with the expectation to be disappointed. Old habits die hard, so don't give up if your needs are not met right away. Keep working on discerning what you really want and finding the courage to ask for it. All the beliefs that have been blocking you will come up in the process, so you can learn to let them go.

As you do this work, you will find many opportunities in your life where you have been living in lack rather than asking for what you need. Whenever you're feeling unhappy or unsatisfied, spend some quiet time alone and ask yourself why. Figure out what you need, open your heart to receiving it, and then go out there and ask for it! Often, you'll find that once you've done your inner work, you don't even need to do the asking anymore. Whatever you were longing for will simply manifest. That's the beauty of the law of attraction. The path truly is the goal.

Exercise

Asking for something that you were denied in the past can fill you with fear of being rejected and having to feel the pain all over again. Be gentle and patient with yourself as you approach this wounded child within you.

It is important to realize that your fear is really just a memory of fear and has no power in the present. Something that had the power to hurt you or scare you when you were five years old need not have the same effect on you as an adult.

Trust yourself to ask and detach from the response. Do a short meditation and ask your highest self to be with you and observe what happens in you, rather than being consumed by whatever feelings arise. Even if it hurts, remember that it's a memory of pain that you are clearing out (e.g., by crying) and not the current situation that is causing the pain. Look at the process of asking as an exercise for your spiritual growth, because as long as you are afraid to ask for what you need, the Universe cannot give it to you.

If you have been living this way for a long time, you may have created some clever excuses for not asking for what you want.

Perhaps you tell yourself that you are just being thoughtful or not wanting to cause any trouble. Perhaps you have disguised your fear as pride or as independence. *Why should I have to ask? They should see that I need help.*

No matter how you disguise your fear, what you are not seeing is that you are standing in your own way. Let go of the clever excuses and start to change what you believe about asking for what you need. I suggest starting with the following affirmations:

It is safe for me to ask for what I need.

My needs matter; I matter.

If this has been an issue in your life, you will likely have strong emotional responses to these affirmations. They will become less intense with time. You need to repeat them as often as possible to allow them to replace your old beliefs. It has been observed that it takes twenty-one uninterrupted days of repeating a new belief to create the new neural pathway in your brain. You'll know this is happening when you feel yourself actually believing what you're affirming!

Once you've changed your belief, you will begin to send out new messages to the Universe that attract new experiences into your life. You will be amazed at the change in how you feel about yourself and how others treat you. Asking may still take some effort at times, but I promise you will find it liberating every time you choose to.

Here are a few examples of situations where people often choose to deny their needs rather than ask for what they want. Do any of these sound like you?

1. You are having dinner at someone's home, and although everyone else seems to be finished eating, you're still hungry. Do you ask for seconds?

2. Again, you're visiting a friend, and you feel cold because the temperature is set so low. Do you say something? If a blanket is offered, do you accept it?

3. In a restaurant, your meal is not quite what you ordered. Do you ask the waiter to correct it or just eat whatever is brought to you?

4. In a meeting, you feel like you're not getting a chance to speak. Do you leave disgruntled or speak up and ask for a turn?

5. Your partner is tired and wants to go to sleep, but you had a hard day and need to talk. Do you let him sleep or ask him for some support?

6. You and your partner have both had long days, and now it's dinnertime. Do you: start preparing something and hope he will help; wait to see if he takes the initiative; get angry that you always have to be responsible for meal planning, or; ask him if he could take care of dinner?

My Story

In early1998, our son was born. Kurt took a week or two off work to help out, and after that, I was on my own with Luke. I didn't mind that. I had always envisioned staying home with my child, and I treasured our time together. Nevertheless, being the mother of an infant is exhausting.

Kurt was at work from about 8:00 a.m. to 7:00 p.m. each day. He usually came home for lunch, but during that time, Luke was often asleep, so it wasn't much help. By the time the weekend came, I longed for some adult interaction with the outside world. Several times I tried, but it never worked out. I would suggest that I go out for a few hours, and Kurt would look at me in dismay. "But I wanted to go for a jog!" he'd say.

I always gave in because I would've felt guilty putting my needs first, although I didn't realize that was the reason at the time. Kurt was used to putting himself first, and I was used to putting myself last. As with many relationships, our neuroses fit perfectly together.

So I agreed that he could go first, and when he got back, I could go. Well, that never happened. I would get busy making us lunch because I knew he'd be hungry when he got back. It was a habit of mine to anticipate and fulfill others' needs—a habit I was stuck in. Then Luke would need to be fed again. By the afternoon, my energy levels dropped, and I felt more like napping with our son than sauntering through the city.

This went on for quite a few months before I realized it was a pattern. It was working out well for Kurt, but I was getting more and more frustrated and even depressed. He didn't seem to care whether I was happy or not, as long as he was getting what he wanted. For me to have even asked for some time for myself was a huge step, but I was not in the habit of requesting something twice if it was rejected the first time. I was still in the beginning stages of changing my beliefs about myself. I was easily convinced that his needs were more important than mine, so I backed down. But now I was starting to feel like it wasn't fair and that he wasn't willing to change anything. At the time, I didn't know what else to do but leave him. Staying in a relationship where I gave until I felt empty and then left, filled with resentment and feeling like a victim, was all part of my own pattern. It certainly didn't make me happy, but it was the only way I knew.

Today I see several other ways I could've managed the situation. I could've talked with him a few days in advance to arrange our Saturdays. I could've let go of the guilt and insisted that it was my turn to have some me time. I could've told him that I would go first. and he could have his jog later. But at that time in my life, I was unable to do any of these things. And my (unconscious) need to be the suffering one would not have been fed if I had.

I had been taught at a very young age that it was not OK to ask for what I needed. My parents were overburdened with other aspects of their lives. If I asked for their time, I was usually disappointed. When I did get some, it had to be shared with—or was snatched away by—my two older sisters. I never got the feeling that I was special. I felt more like I was in the way—a burden. I'm sure that, financially at least, I was one. So I got used to being tolerated on the best of days and rejected on the worst. I developed the survival strategy of not making waves, lying low, and not causing any trouble. Always wanting more than I got became familiar territory—one I would continue to create for many years to come.

Those were the beliefs I took with me into my marriage. *Thanks for putting up with me. I don't want to be any trouble. Please don't leave me! No, no, you go ahead. I'll just wait here until it's more convenient for you. Sorry. Sorry for being here. Sorry for being in the way. Sorry for being.*

It took a lot of work to get from there to where I am today. Every day, I'm getting better at identifying and asking for what I need. And the best part of changing those beliefs is that I am now open to receiving it all without feeling guilty! And if I ask and the answer is no, I don't take it as a personal rejection or a confirmation that I am not worthy. Instead, I look for where I might still have a belief that's blocking me—and I always find one! Today, with a healthy sense of self, I can accept that my needs don't have to always be met in order for me to believe that I'm important to someone. I feel safe enough to ask because I know now that I matter.

Asking

Many of us know the suffering that arises when we look to our significant others to fill our needs. How can they when all the information we give them is "I'm not happy. You are at fault." We desperately want them to make us feel better, but even if they manage to for a brief moment, it can't last. The emptiness is our own. We need to fix it ourselves. We need to learn to give to ourselves what was missing in our childhoods, and in that process, we will remove the blocks we've set up. That's when we will learn that it's safe to ask for it again. Now that we've opened our hearts to receive that loving attention we missed out on, we can ask for it. If we are truly open, it will come. It has to. It's the law of attraction.

Instead, what we more often do is put the ridiculous expectation on our romantic partners to fill this void without telling them what we really need. We can't tell them because we haven't done the work of identifying what it is. So, instead, we criticize them for who they are and find fault in all they do, because the truth is we are not open to receiving what we need from them. How fair does that seem? We are angry with our partners for not giving us something that we are not aware we need, not asking for, and not open to receiving. Unless your partner is clairvoyant, you are not likely to have much success with this approach.

The next time you feel unfulfilled and want to blame your partner, look in the mirror instead. Try a simple meditation and just ask yourself what you need. If it's something you can give yourself, like self-care or simply rest, do it. If it's something you feel you need from your partner, ask for it without any accusation or expectation. Remember, if it doesn't come, it's because you're still blocking, so get to work on yourself, and your relationship will satisfy your every desire.

DESERVING

We give up a lot of joy because we don't think we deserve it.
—Joyce Meyer

When you begin to ask for what you want in life, you will come face-to-face with whether or not you feel that you deserve it. In many cases, this is a major block. And as with most of the things that are blocking our happiness, we are often not aware of it.

Do you believe that you deserve to be treated with love and respect? Most of us would answer yes to this question. Who doesn't want to be treated well? Many of us complain that we don't get the respect we deserve, but even though we say this, we may not really believe that we are worthy enough to deserve it. One of the easiest ways to see if you truly feel deserving is to look at your current relationships.

If one of your friends has a habit of treating you with less respect than they should, what do you do? Let's say you know that they are gossiping about you or comparing themselves and competing with you in some way. Maybe they let little put-downs slip out and call them jokes. Would you still consider that person a friend?

What if a family member was manipulating you and belittling your thoughts and feelings? What if they refused to acknowledge your successes but seemed to enjoy reminding you of your failures? Would you just let it go or would you say something? A lot of the time, we make excuses for family members who mistreat us. "Oh, that's just the way she is. She doesn't mean it!"

In reality, we are just afraid to stand up for ourselves. The first thing to be aware of is that something about the way you see yourself is attracting these relationships. You can't change the other person if you aren't willing to look at yourself. Maybe long ago you decided that it was easier to see yourself as the problem than to admit to yourself that your caregiver, parent, or older sibling was less than perfect? It can be scary to think that those we are depending on do not have our best interest at heart, so we convince ourselves that the way they are treating us must be the way we deserve to be treated.

This pattern follows us into our adult lives and repeats itself until we finally say, "Stop." We find ourselves unfulfilled, unappreciated, or even abused in our relationships, and too often, we resign ourselves to expecting nothing more, because we don't feel we deserve any better. You have to start by treating yourself better, which might mean standing up to or walking away from a person in your life who is not treating you well.

Every behavior you tolerate from others is a message to the Universe about what you feel you deserve. If you stay in these relationships as they are, you are telling the Universe that you deserve to be gossiped about, competed with rather than supported, and criticized. You are sending out the message that it's OK for your feelings to be ignored and for you to be used and manipulated for the needs of others. Then you wonder why people keep treating you like this.

There can be many examples of situations like these going on in your life without your realizing it, because you've never know any other way. We often don't see how unhealthy our relationships are because we have nothing to compare them with. We might see others in healthier relationships, but we can't imagine that for ourselves. It's unfamiliar. Sadly, we often choose to stay with what's familiar, even when it makes us unhappy. Sometimes we purposely turn a blind eye to the way we are being treated, because we fear the upheaval in our lives if we were to take a stand. And maybe deep down, we just don't believe that we deserve any better.

My Story

It was my thirty-third birthday. Our son was three months old. None of the five birthdays I spent with Kurt were what I'd hoped for, but this one took the cake, so to speak. As we woke up that morning, he handed me a watch. It was not wrapped, and there was no card. It was a nice watch; I'll give him that. Better than the cookbooks he'd given me the two years prior. I thanked him, and we got out of bed. I went to check on Luke. As I was feeding and changing him, I thought Kurt might be making me a nice breakfast. That was what I would've been doing if it had been the other way around, but no such luck. When I came out into the living room, I found him watching TV. I said nothing and started preparing breakfast. I was disappointed, to be sure, but I said nothing. Perhaps there was a part of me that felt comfortable in the role of the martyr.

As the day went on, it felt like any other day. Nothing special. I quietly hoped that he had something special planned for dinner. Perhaps a surprise? As the afternoon wore on, nothing he said or did indicated that he had a plan. Still, I hoped but said nothing.

Our usual dinner time arrived, and he was still watching TV. By now, my hopes were so crushed I felt physically heavy. I managed to ask him if he was hungry, hoping to offer an opening to a spontaneous idea at this point. He said no; he'd had a big snack not long before.

So I dragged myself into the kitchen and tried to find something to eat. There was not much in the fridge, as I expected not to be cooking that night. I managed to find a package of instant soup mix. The part of me that believed I deserved nothing more than this was reveling in the pity party. I made the soup and ate it at the table alone, holding back the tears as he continued to watch TV.

That was it. That was my thirty-third. Before I learned that I create my own reality. Before I understood what I deserved. Before I opened my arms wide and declared to the *Universe* that I deserve to be happy!

Gradually over the years that followed, I made the effort to make the day special for myself in various ways. If you want someone to make you feel special, you've got to start treating yourself that way! I walked away from my marriage because I blamed Kurt for not making me feel special, but I didn't see at the time that it had to start with me. He couldn't give me anything I was convinced I didn't deserve. I was the one who had to change. I had to throw away my martyr hat and change my story.

On my own with my son for my thirty-fourth, I invited friends over for an elaborate brunch—champagne and all! They all came, bearing gifts, and stayed for hours, celebrating my new life with me! I was learning to love myself and to give myself the special treatment that I had longed for from others, and it was reflecting back in the way they treated me.

Now that I've done the inner work and learned that I am special, valuable, and deserve to be treated like a princess, I've allowed a partner into my life who reflects that. I've traded in my martyr hat for a tiara, and I'm loving it!

Exercise

Answer these questions in your journal or notebook. It is important to actually write out your answers, not just think about them.

- How do you allow others to treat you? Why? What holds you back from standing up and saying no (guilt, fear of losing them, etc.)?
- What kind of patterns do you see in your relationships? Are you always the one who gives in? The one who gets burnt? Feels used?
- Have you been asking for a loving partner yet feeling deep down that you are not good enough? Do you tend to fall for people who are not available?
- Have you been asking for a healthy body but have a deep-seated belief that you don't deserve it because you watched your parents suffer so much with their health?
- Are you hoping to find a fulfilling job but feel like you should settle because no one around you likes their job either?
- What messages did you get about deserving as a child?
- Did your parents tell you that you deserve to be happy and fulfilled, or did they model an existence of suffering and struggle?
- How deserving do you think your parents felt? What about their parents?
- Do you believe that you deserve to be happy? Healthy? Prosperous? At peace? Why or why not?

Doing this exercise can be very difficult. Many of us were not given positive messages about what kind of life we deserve to be living, and it can be very sobering to see them right there in black and white.

The good news is that by uncovering these beliefs about deserving, you take away some of the power they've had over your life. You've already weakened those beliefs. Now it's time to change them altogether!

It doesn't matter how long you've believed these things; you can choose to change them now! Now go back through all that you have written and replace any negative messages about what you deserve with positive ones. Pick the positive affirmation that seems most difficult to say and write it out on a separate page in bold print.

Hold it in your hand or place it where you can see it and do a short meditation. Close your eyes and count five deep breaths in and out. Then, with your next in breath, say the affirmation in your mind. Repeat it at least ten times, in sync with your in breath. Now open your eyes and notice how you feel.

When you've finished the meditation, record all critical, opposing voices that came up, so that you can take away their power too. Remember, what we aren't aware of is influencing our lives much more than our conscious thoughts, so making the unconscious thoughts conscious will weaken them over time.

As well, repetition of your new, chosen thoughts on how deserving you are will make them stronger, so write them down and stick them on the wall or mirror, in the car, where you'll see them. Say them out loud as you're showering or driving to work.

Most importantly, take the time to repeat them in meditation for a few minutes a day. This is the most effective way to embed new beliefs about what you deserve into your subconscious mind, increasing your power to attract wonderful, healthy experiences and relationships into your life!

It's Not What You Do; It's Why You Do It

You might think that helping someone out is a positive thing, so doing so should bring you something positive. Let's say you're in charge of shining the statues on the altar at your temple or setting things up for communion at your church. These seem like very good works that would make you worthy of blessings, right?

It's not that simple. Once I had the experience of helping someone as he was polishing the candle holders in the temple I was visiting. We had just had satsung, which means chanting, meditating, and sharing wisdom teachings. Now we were cleaning up, and he asked me if I would help him with this task. I happily agreed. For me, it was a labor of love and gratitude, as the prayers had left me feeling at peace and filled with love.

This person, however, was grumbling the whole time. "Nobody else ever does this. All the work always lands on the same few people. Why doesn't anyone else ever see what needs to be done?"

I said nothing, but I felt very sorry for this person. I saw that in his mind, he was doing good works for God, and he truly felt that he would be rewarded for this. According to the law of attraction, however, his negative feelings about what he was doing would block anything positive from getting in.

The same action can be done out of love or out of fear. A person can steal to feed their starving child or simply out of greed or envy. It can't be the action that sends the energy out to the Universe because the same action can be positive in one case and negative in another. It's got to be the motivation behind the action or the feeling we have while doing it that creates the vibrational message we emit.

In short, don't waste your time on good works if your heart is not in it. You're not really helping the other person/people, and you're certainly not helping yourself. When you give, give joyfully, and you'll attract much more to be joyful about.

BELIEFS

Belief indicates a life that is based on make-believe, which has nothing to do with actuality.
—J. Krishnamurti

What do you believe? When we are little children, we are wide open. If a trusted adult tells us that a man in a red suit comes down our chimney on Christmas Eve and leaves us all a pile of presents, we believe it. A cynic might say that's because children are gullible. The truth, however, is that in the mind of a child, *all things are possible*. That's not only a beautiful thing; it's also a powerful one.

As we grow up, the adults in our lives feed us their beliefs about ourselves and the world, and we accept all of it. We wouldn't think of questioning what they tell us, because we are so trusting and innocent. So, if they tell us that we are smart, creative, beautiful, or loved, we believe that. Unfortunately, if they tell us that we are lazy, no good, stupid, or ugly, we believe that too.

Some beliefs we adopt have to do with outer things, like the world, work, the opposite sex, our bodies, and money. And they don't always come from our parents. They can come from other adults in our lives, older siblings, or even advertising. Commonly held beliefs in the specific culture we grow up in are some of the most difficult to root out, because if everyone believes them, we have nothing to offer us a contrast.

That's why it's so easy to look at and criticize the beliefs of another culture while remaining blind to our own. For example, people from the Western world often criticize the way women are treated in other areas of the world, but in the days when Western women were not allowed to vote or were expected to be the subservient housewives, most of us were not able to see that there was anything wrong with that.

We believe what we are told, what we learn to believe through example, and what we absorb through our cultures. And we take for granted that these things are true, sometimes with very painful or even tragic results. The beliefs we hold limit the experiences that we allow ourselves to attract into our lives.

I know of a woman whose father told her repeatedly that she would end up being a stripper or flipping burgers, because that's all she was good for. His statement had nothing to do with the truth of the value of this beautiful girl, but she was too young to know that. She, like all of us, internalized and believed what her father told her. Sure enough, this young girl found herself dancing in strip clubs in her late teens. He said it, she believed it, and it manifested. That's an obvious example, but often the beliefs that sabotage our lives are far more subtle.

Our beliefs become a part of us that we take with us everywhere we go. They are like tapes playing in our subconscious minds, but they've been playing for so long they're like white noise in the background. We barely even notice all the self-critical, self-sabotaging talk that is constantly playing in our heads. These thoughts, however, are powerful energy, and without being aware of it, we are sending that negative energy out into the Universe. What comes back to us in our physical world, of course, matches this energy.

For example, if you had a mother who was unhappy or angry with your father for any reason, you might've heard phrases like "men are no good," "all men want is one thing," or "men are jerks" (or worse) as you were growing up. These phrases became a part of your mental tapes, and you may not have realized it.

Even if you didn't like hearing it, never agreed with your mom, and are truly hoping to meet a nice and caring guy, chances are high that every guy who gets close to you ends up fulfilling one of the above statements.

"Why do I keep attracting the same kind of partner?" is a question many people have asked me. In fact, I used to ask it myself.

You need to become more aware of your underlying beliefs so that you can change them. The fact is that your reality in the external world will always arrange itself to fit your internal reality. So, no matter how different a new partner may seem, you'll always wind up stuck in the same old role unless you do the inner work.

What we need to realize is that there is no truth to our beliefs. They were someone else's opinions, and we agreed to adopt them as our own. We have a lot of resistance to letting them go because they feel like the truth to us, but they're not. When you accept this and are willing to let go of your beliefs, your life will begin to transform in wonderful and exciting ways.

But changing our beliefs is possible only if we are aware of them. We each have so many of them hiding in the back of our minds and creating all the undesirable situations in our lives. The only way to take away their power is to bring them out of the darkness and into the light.

Meditation is a very helpful tool in this.

Exercise

Do a short breath-awareness meditation before finishing the following sentences. Just take ten conscious, slow breaths with the intention of uncovering your negative beliefs. Now let's have a look at some of the beliefs you have been carrying with you so far in life. As honestly as you can, without worrying about political correctness, finish the following phrases:

1. Men are _____.
2. Women are _____.
3. Rich people are _____.
4. Life is _____.
5. People should _____.
6. There's not enough _____.
7. Poor people _____.
8. Love is _____.
9. I am _____.
10. The world is _____.

Now go back over your answers and put a star beside the ones that are negative. Does it surprise you to see how many are? Don't worry if it's all of them! The more negative stuff that comes up now, the more you can clean it up!

It's important that you be very honest with yourself as you fill in the blanks. If you cover up your negative beliefs and write down "nice" answers, you will lose all the benefit of the exercise. (If you think you did that, go back and do the exercise again.)

We are trying to shed light on negative messages that you have been unconsciously sending out into the Universe so that you can change them. If you don't allow them into your consciousness, the negative beliefs will continue to show up in your physical reality. Only by becoming aware that you are carrying a belief can you begin to change it.

Any thought that we think over and over again creates a neural pathway in our brain, like a groove in a dirt road made by tires going over it again and again. Over time, the thought becomes like a habit, just as tires would tend to easily slip into the grooves that are already there, rather than create new ones.

But the key is that we *can* create new ones! Studies have shown that by repeating new and more life-enhancing thoughts, we can rewire our brains so that our mind chatter becomes more positive. This means that even the thoughts we are not consciously aware of throughout the day will begin to attract more positive energy into our lives.

Now look at each negative belief you've uncovered and choose a positive thought or affirmation to replace it. If you wrote, "Men are liars," try "Men are honest." "There's not enough time" could become "There is plenty of time for me to get everything done that I need to!"

It's completely within your power to change each and every negative belief that has been lurking in your mind, no matter how long it's been there. Just change what you thought was true into what you'd like to have as your reality and repeat it as often as possible.

As Henry David Thoreau said:

> As a single footstep will not make a path on the earth, so a single thought will not make a pathway in the mind. To make a deep physical path, we walk again and again. To make a deep mental path, we must think over and over the kind of thoughts we wish to dominate our lives.

Next, we'll go into a meditation so that we can introduce your new beliefs to your heart, mind, and body. Repeating these thoughts in your normal waking state is definitely helpful, but saying them in your mind during meditation makes the message sink into your whole being that much faster.

Meditation: Close your eyes and focus on your breath. Just observe the flow of breath, and if you like, count them. Counting your breaths is a simple way to keep your mind from wandering. After a minute or two of conscious breathing, start to say your affirmations in your mind. You can choose one or several each time. I suggest focussing on a maximum of five affirmations in one sitting and repeating them three times each, in rhythm with your breaths.

When you're done, you can journal about which thoughts offered the most resistance, what felt silly to say, and what brought up the most resistance or fear. These are the affirmations that you need to work on most. Keep repeating them. Write them down and stick them on your mirror or in your car—anywhere you will see them often. Depending on how long and how deeply you've believed the negative thought, it could take a while before you notice a change. But if you stick with it, I promise you will eventually feel a shift happen. Not only will you feel better, because your energy is more positive, but you will also see proof in the people and situations you attract.

My Story

When I was a little girl, I idolized my father, as most little girls do. He had his positive sides, but overall, my experience of him made me into a fearful and insecure person. My father struggled with his own inner demons, and sometimes they got the better of him.

Sometimes he was the modern parent, willing to discuss and debate with his kids, encouraging us to speak up and voice our opinions. Other times, he would be the authoritarian, pounding his fist on the table and yelling, "Because I said so!" He had an unpredictable temper, and I never knew what might set him off. Like most kids, I blamed myself if he got angry. I was too young to understand that his moods had nothing to do with me. I took on the responsibility of keeping him happy—being the good, obedient girl so that I would not have to experience his unpredictable fits of rage.

Without my realizing it, all of these experiences shaped the beliefs I developed around men, safety, love, power, and, of course, myself. I got used to walking on eggshells with my father; used to being the emotional caregiver. My own happiness came second. I was focused on taking care of his needs first, and they were many.

The man I ended up marrying seemed quite different from my father at first. Kurt was financially stable, for one thing. He seemed more motivated to take care of his own health, doing triathlons regularly. He presented himself as a modern, emancipated man who was interested in an equal partnership. But as time went on, he reminded me more and more of my father.

His unpredictable temper was the first similarity. It didn't surprise me. It was all too familiar for me to walk on eggshells so as not to set him off. In a way, I expected it. This, of course, gave him power over me, and he used it to control me in many ways.

Since it was my belief that men were authority figures, and I grew up afraid of making my father angry with me, I could only be attracted to a man who would fit that description.

As the years went by, this man who I thought was my Prince Charming turned into my worst nightmare. He didn't care whether I was happy or not, as long as his needs were being filled. A few months after our son was born, I recall telling him how lonely and unhappy I felt in France. He got angry with me and accused me of not trying hard enough to meet people. No compassion, no support. I was feeling depressed and had a three-month-old baby. There was not much energy left for meeting people. And even if I did, my self-esteem was so low that

I couldn't imagine anyone wanting to spend time with me. It's hard to make new friends when you feel worthless, which was the result of his constant criticism.

Kurt became ever more controlling, moody, and unpredictable. No matter what I did for him, it never seemed to be enough. I had left behind all my friends in Germany to be with him. He never liked me spending time with them. He was incredibly jealous and possessive, to the point that if I was on the phone with a friend or family member when he got home from work and did not immediately end the call to pay attention to him, he would not speak to me for the rest of the evening. He needed me to live for him and only him—to need him and no one else. So I gave up my entire life in Germany to prove to him that I loved him, but it didn't work.

I had been trying to make him happy for five years when it dawned on me one day that I would never succeed. I had nothing left to give, yet it still wasn't enough. I wasn't enough. My love wasn't enough. There was nothing more I could do. I was emotionally drained, yet he was still demanding. I couldn't just live my own life with him. He needed my constant attention and care. I had to cheer him on in every sports event he entered. I had to have a hot meal ready whenever he came home from work. I had to be there when he called. I couldn't even nap when he was home, or he would complain and call me lazy.

It would have been all too easy to just walk away feeling like a victim, yet again, and blame it all on him. But I'd walked away from two other long-term relationships before, and I was desperate to end this pattern. I couldn't believe another relationship was ending after a few years, with me feeling drained, brokenhearted, and resentful. Why, when they all seemed to start off so well, did it always feel like that at the end? What was I not seeing? I didn't have the energy to keep that up every few years. I needed to find out why it was happening and stop it.

It was then, in 1999, that I started learning about the law of attraction. I was reading books by Louise Hay and Iyanla Vanzant, which helped me understand my role in attracting these relationships. My eyes were opening to the connection between the men I'd been drawn to and the man I called Father.

As I continued to meditate and uncover my beliefs about men and love, I understood completely how my energy had attracted this man who treated me the way I was used to being treated. (Of course, his energy attracted a person who he could easily manipulate and control as well; it works both ways.) Even if I didn't like it, I was not capable of being in any other kind of relationship at the time. The tapes playing in my head said this was the way things had to be for me. It was the only way I knew to be in a partnership, and in its own strange way, it felt safe, because it was familiar. The ego likes familiarity. Being in that marriage was not threatening to my ego, but it was starving my soul.

I was in no rush to be in another relationship after I left my marriage. I was happy just to have my own four walls with my little boy, who was one year old. I was learning that I didn't need to have a man at my side to prove to the world that I was worthy of love. I was finally, gradually, learning to love myself, and this was a huge step in taking back my power.

As the years went by, I did have a few short-term companions. As much as I wanted to be ready for *the one*, these men were stepping-stones in my journey. Each of them mirrored to me the way I was changing. I no longer attracted egotistical men. Each one was kinder, more thoughtful than the last. Sometimes they challenged me with old patterns, and it was up to me to respond in a different way, such as speaking up and not being afraid to put my needs first. I had to learn not to give my power away, and it took quite a few years of practice, but it certainly has been worth it.

Abuse

It's important to be clear here: if you are in an abusive relationship, I am not saying that it's your fault because you attracted it. You did attract it—but not on purpose. The unconscious beliefs that attract us to unhealthy connections today were embedded in us long ago, likely through abusive relationships in our childhood.

We don't realize these beliefs are there, so how could it be our fault that we've "chosen" an abusive partner? Others may have warned us against marrying this person, but we couldn't see it. Why not? We don't notice that anything's wrong because what we knew as normal was so messed up. That's not our fault. That's the fault of those whose care we were in as children. They failed to demonstrate to us what healthy relationships look like—what real love feels like.

Now we've got these false beliefs about ourselves lurking in the back of our minds, and without us realizing it, they're determining our fate. It's like we think we're driving the car, but in reality, our steering wheel isn't even connected. It's on autopilot. A part of us that we aren't aware of is making the decisions, often despite our better judgment.

I often hear people judging others for staying in abusive relationships. Nothing could be more unjust than this. It's easy to see from the outside—outside the conditioning—that a relationship is unhealthy. But judging, shaming, and getting frustrated with the victim of abuse who is not ready to leave her abuser is never going to help.

It's important to understand this if you know someone who is being abused. They need your unconditional love and support. They need to know that there is a safe place for them to run to when they are ready, and they need you to be patient and wait until they are. It's got to come from inside them if it is going to work. Each of us has to come to a point where we know—with a deep certainty—that things can no longer be the way they have been up to now. We don't need to know what the future will look like; we just need to know that we're done with the past.

We won't find happiness by leaving one relationship and looking for a "better" partner right away. Until we've worked through the reasons why we attracted an abusive partner in the first place, we will continue to attract more of the same. Change begins within. Look honestly at your past and uncover the truth about your childhood relationships. Only then can you let go of old beliefs, start over, and choose new, healthier ones.

PAIN

*If someone comes along and shoots an arrow into
your heart, it's fruitless to stand there and yell at the
person. It would be much better to turn your attention
to the fact that there's an arrow in your heart.*

—Pema Chodron

Everyone has pain. Some of us are more aware of our pain than others, but unless you've been surrounded by perfect people all your life, whether you know it or not, you've got some.

Pain is one of those things that we often try to hide from. That's where drugs, alcohol, gambling, shopping, binge eating, running, working, and the like come in handy. Everyone's got an addiction of some kind—a coping mechanism that they learned long ago in order to keep those unbearable feelings locked up.

Unfortunately, if we keep the feelings down, they clog up our pipes, as it were. I've described this in my classes as "sludge." When your pipes are clogged with sludge, the water will not flow through them as freely as it could. Unclogging them is, of course, not pretty. You have to reach inside and pull out the clump of slimy, hairy mess that is stuck inside. The longer it's been there, the bigger and messier it is. As you're pulling it out, it might smell so bad that you might want to run out of the room. You might want to hide from it all, pretend it's not there, or hope that someone else will unclog it for you.

But that's not going to happen. The longer you wait, the more clogged your pipes are going to be, and you're the only one who can clear them. You can wait until the water stops flowing altogether, until the drain backs up and it overflows all over the floor and messes everything up.

That's what happens often. We wait until the emotional pain we've been carrying just overflows into our physical selves, and then there's no more ignoring it! That headache, back pain, or arthritis is not going to just disappear on its own. But wait! We still have the option of hoping someone else can fix us! To the doctor we go, and here come the painkillers. Have you ever noticed that people on pain medication are constantly needing to increase the dosage or strength of their medication? Have you ever wondered why?

It's because your pain is going to let you know it's there, one way or another. If you won't listen to what it's saying to you, it will have to raise its voice until it is heard, even if it has to scream!

The same applies to any addictive habits we use to help us ignore our pain. We'll need more and more to keep it down as the years go by.

The only way of finally silencing the pain is to stop all the busyness, sit quietly, and listen to it.

Exercise

Have a box of tissues nearby and a pen and paper. You may wish to light a candle and/or say a prayer before beginning this exercise. Ask for guidance, support, and strength. Above all, know that you are not alone as you take this courageous step. When we work toward our wholeness, we are always supported by the Universe. Let yourself feel that support by opening up with a few deep breaths.

Now, think of a painful event from your past. As unpleasant as it may feel, allow yourself to write about it in detail. Write what happened, how you felt at the time, and how you wished things could've been different. Let your tears flow, trusting that this is a powerful and important cleansing of your energy. Sob, scream, wail—whatever you need to release this pain from your mind/body.

When you are finished, thank the Universe for helping you to heal in this way. Then, do something nice for yourself: take a bath, take a walk in nature, have a nap … whatever your heart needs after this powerful release.

You will need to repeat this exercise regularly. Pace yourself and don't let yourself get frustrated. You may be surprised to see just how much pain you've been carrying around with you, but the good news is, every time you notice more pain, it's on its way out of you forever!

My Story

The sad part about growing up in a family where you don't feel seen is that you continue to attract people into your life who follow this pattern. If I had known twenty years ago that the way people perceived me and treated me had more to do with them than me, I could've saved myself a lot of heartache.

I let it affect my self-esteem that my boyfriends cheated on me. I asked myself what was wrong with me that they were drawn to other women. What I should've been asking was, what was wrong with them?

When Kurt came along, the physical attraction was not as much in the foreground as it had been with former partners. I thought that was a good thing, since we are always being warned not to confuse sex with love. This was not all about sex, so I assumed, by default, it must be more about love. Mistake number one. After the first six months, the frequency of our lovemaking began to decrease. Again, I tried to tell myself that this was OK, that our love was somehow deeper than others', and therefore we didn't need to have sex that often. Or maybe we were just having a dry spell and things would pick up again soon.

The ego is good at creating excuses. When Kurt came home from a two-week-long business trip, however, and nothing happened, I was very confused. I couldn't find an explanation for this. With any other partner, we would've been longing for each other after the break! I expected a passionate reunion, but all I got was a hello and a hug. I should have seen then that there was a bigger problem, but I was likely afraid to. I so desperately wanted this relationship to be the one. I naively hoped that it would all work itself out in time. In retrospect, I should've known when he told me that in the four-year-long relationship he'd had before ours, there had been no sex at all, that something was seriously wrong.

I was an attractive woman in my late twenties. I got enough male attention to know that. But the one I had promised my fidelity to was not attracted to me. I tried to talk to him several times, but he blamed me, criticized my body, or said I was pressuring him too much. As the years passed, it just got worse. When I broached the subject, which was not often, he promised that he would deal with it and asked me to be patient. More years passed, and instead of seeing any increase in our intimacy, it gradually faded away almost entirely. Sometimes I tried to initiate, but after a little cuddling, he'd turn his back to me and say good night.

I felt rejected and undesirable. Many times, I lay beside him with my back facing his, crying myself quietly to sleep. In our last year together, we had sex twice. I was a thirty-two-year-old woman with a healthy, normal sexual appetite, but he made me feel like something was wrong with me, and I believed him. Of course, there are other ways to experience the intimacy I longed for. Even just looking deeply into another's eyes can be an intimate experience. But we didn't have that either. In fact, even in talks, I felt I could be more open with friends—male and female—than with Kurt. Why had I chosen to marry this man when there were others I got along so much better with? Trusted more? Could be more open with?

I have learned the hard way that injuries of a sexual nature, whether abuse, infidelity, or rejection, cut very deep. Our most intimate and vulnerable selves are damaged, and what makes it worse, it is often very difficult to talk about with others.

That's why I chose this story to share. I am sure there are others suffering in silence, as I did in those years. I want you to know right now: there's nothing wrong with you!

Kurt became more and more critical of many things about me over our five years together. He started out loving everything about me, and by the fifth year, I honestly wondered why he was still with me because he didn't seem to like anything about me. Nothing! He criticized the way I walked, the way I spoke, the way I ate. There was never a kind or encouraging word for the mother of his child. Instead, he seemed to want to compete with me and show me that he was the better parent. Every day, he wore me down more, until I finally crawled away—a mere shadow of the woman I'd been five years earlier.

What I see today is that I obviously did not see or appreciate myself. If I had, I'd have never been attracted to his energy. I chose him because I knew he would not let me get too close. I could blame the lack of intimacy on him, but the truth was I was afraid to open myself as much as he was. The years of criticism and rejection mirrored back to me what I had not wanted to look at. I really didn't feel worthy of love. I felt ugly and unwanted inside, and I couldn't let anyone get too close, lest they discover that. It would take me another few years to understand this and even longer to heal the wounds that had caused me to feel that way.

I also understand now that Kurt didn't like himself much either; like attracts like. You can never truly love someone else when you don't even like yourself. I was fighting a losing battle, trying to win his love and approval. I would never be enough because, in reality, he was not even seeing me. How could he ever love me?

What I've come to see is that he most likely didn't want a woman at all. I wonder how many men are denying their true nature and marrying women to avoid losing love and approval? No wonder he grew to dislike everything about me no matter what I did. I could never be what he wanted because what he wanted was a man. It took me a while to realize this was the reason my husband would not sleep with me, and it took even longer to heal the deep wounds of years of rejection that the experience left me with.

It has been a gradual process of peeling away the layers of deep pain since I left Kurt, like an onion (tears and all!). Any time I was able to open my heart and let a little more love in, I also noticed pain going out. I gradually shifted the balance of energies within me and was thrilled one day in meditation to realize that I could truly feel unconditional love for myself! I felt how beautiful and loved I was and how much I loved the person I was becoming. In fact, I was remembering the truth about myself—who I was before all the negative conditioning and painful experiences told me I was less. I was remembering my worth. It was amazing.

Some memories of pain can be dealt with quicker than others. My experience is that the longer we suppress the pain, the longer it takes to process it when we finally do. So start now! The sooner you begin to acknowledge and release your pain, the sooner you will clear those pipes and allow more wonderful things to flow into your life!

Meditation

Sit with the pain.

Simply sit quietly, breathe consciously, and talk to your pain. Tell your pain that you acknowledge its presence and that you are not going to ignore it or try to push it back down anymore. Ask your pain what it is there to tell you. Take deep breaths and pay attention to the thoughts or memories that come up. As they do, acknowledge and release them. Give your body permission to let go of the physical pain and breathe it out.

You can do this on a regular basis (e.g., once a week) or simply follow your body's guidance: when you feel any pain at all, know that your soul is trying to tell you something through your body and meditate to learn what it is!

You might want to journal any insights you receive about your pain. Writing helps us to let go of things that meditation has brought to the surface.

GUILT

*Dear God ... Heal my guilt and remove
my anger, that I might be reborn.*
—Marianne Williamson

There's nothing positive about guilt. Fear and anger have their place; they are necessary reactions to certain situations, if expressed in a healthy manner. But guilt? I see no positive side to this feeling. Some people confuse guilt with having a conscience. To me, these are two separate things.

A conscience is my guide in living according to the morals and values that I believe in. It helps me live a life of integrity. Guilt is closer to fear than integrity. It causes us to act based on a fear of being punished or judged.

It can be true in some cases, I suppose, that guilt motivates us to do something good, like buying fair trade coffee. For example, if I buy the coffee that was cheaper (because the farmers were exploited), I may feel guilty afterward, and that could influence me to buy fair trade the next time.

But here's the catch: guilt is very close to fear in its vibration. Remember that everything boils down to a choice between fear and love. Doing something motivated by guilt is not going to attract anything positive into your life; it only gives the guilt a stronger hold on you.

It would be better to buy the fair trade coffee out of love for humanity and the recognition that we are all connected. If one of us is suffering, we are all suffering. If one of us is healing, we are all healing. If that heart awakening is the motivation for making the more ethical choice, it will allow more positive energy into your life.

It's not the action itself. It's the intention behind the action that matters. We need to learn to examine our feelings to determine what is motivating our actions; otherwise, we could be shooting ourselves in the foot while thinking we're doing "the right thing." We often tell ourselves that we are doing something out of love when in reality it is guilt—fear of upsetting/ hurting/disappointing someone. Guilt is an epidemic in our society, and the most challenging part about it is that people don't realize how much it is controlling them.

I once had a client—a well-educated woman—who, when I brought up the topic of guilt in one of my meditation groups, said to me with pride, "I have no guilt." She was a very kind and giving person and always felt stretched to the limit in trying to please all the people in her life. Everyone had demands (or requests) of her, and she hated to let them down. Every time I spoke with her, for years she would say, "Something's gotta give! I can't do this anymore!" She pushed herself to the point of exhaustion, trying to make those around her happy. Fortunately, she continued to meditate regularly, and she gradually began to see that her frustration and exhaustion were the result of not being able to say no, and that guilt was the reason. Meditation is a very effective way of seeing the things we are living in denial about. You can't change a behaviour if you don't see it.

Whenever we do something out of guilt, we inevitably resent having done it. We may tell ourselves that we are OK with it at the time, but if guilt was the motivator, resentment will eventually follow. Think of someone you resent right now. Why do you resent them? If you are able to dig deep enough, chances are you'll realize that you often do things for this person out of guilt. We blame them, but we're the ones who keep on doing it. Learning to say no will help us to break this cycle, but it will bring up guilt if we're used to people pleasing.

Sometimes we notice that we feel angry toward someone, but we don't realize that it's because we feel manipulated into doing things for them that we don't want to. We resent them because we were not able to say no. Very often, we pour more judgment on ourselves for this anger, rather than acknowledging it as a valid feeling under the circumstances. We act out of guilt, get angry, and then judge ourselves for it. That's a whole lot of negative energy.

As long as we don't get a handle on our guilt, we will attract people who will use it to manipulate us. It's our energy that's attracting theirs, but we rarely see that. People who are driven by guilt have a certain energy. In their family of origin, where the pattern likely began, they may have been programmed to be caregivers, so as adults, they continue to put the needs of others before their own.

Do you get frustrated by people in your life manipulating you? Have you tried to change them? Asked them to stop? Complained or gossiped about them? Blown up at them?

Often, controlling people use guilt as a way to maintain the power that they have over you. That's what makes it so difficult for adult children, for example, to stand up to their parents.

Let's say one of your parents is constantly picking at you, criticizing you in subtle ways for the way you dress, the amount you eat, or something else. It hurts your feelings, embarrasses you in front of others, and leaves you feeling like a helpless, frustrated child every time. You muster up all your courage and finally say, "Mom, it bothers me when you criticize me for …"

And suddenly this all-powerful being appears wounded to the core. "I was only trying to help you. How can you be so ungrateful? If it wasn't for me, you would be …" and so on. Sometimes it's more subtle. Sometimes they just clam up, walk away, or turn to stone. No matter what method they use, the message is the same: *you have hurt me.* (Never mind how much they have been hurting you for years—and you just kept taking it.)

All your efforts to stand up for yourself are now buried under the heaviness of guilt. So often we then backtrack, apologize profusely, or do something to make it up somehow. If they grace us with "forgiveness," then we reenter into the pattern of manipulation and guilt. This pattern can go on for years if we don't do the work we need to do to break free of guilt.

In my work with clients over the years, it's safe to say that 90 percent of the issues they are struggling with are rooted in guilt toward one or both of their parents. It doesn't matter if the parent is alive or dead either. Their voices live on in our heads long after they're gone. They become our beliefs.

It is possible to become aware of these voices, which is the first step in changing them. Meditation will help you recognize when guilt is holding you back from saying what you need to say or otherwise setting your healthy boundaries. Believe it or not, it is possible to not attend that family gathering and still be a worthy human being! But you have to release the guilt if you want to survive the judgment. When guilt no longer has a hold on you, others can go on playing their mind games, and it will no longer affect you. They will no longer get a reaction out of you, so they'll move on and let you be. This is how you take your power back. When you stop reacting, the manipulators in your life will have to look elsewhere to feed their need to control others.

Guilt is an energy like everything else, and we can learn to free ourselves from it so that we can set our healthy limits with people and give ourselves permission to say no.

Exercise: EFT for Guilt

Karate chop point: "Even though I'm feeling guilty about_____, I deeply and completely love and accept myself." (Three times.)

Then tap through the other points, saying:

First round: "This guilt. All this guilt. I feel so guilty." (Repeat through all points.)

Second round: (Describe the situation). For example, "If I say no to this person, they will be so disappointed; if I don't help them, they will suffer; it would be selfish of me to not help."

(Describe your biggest fear). For example, "If I don't step in and do this for them, they could die! And it would be my fault! I would feel so guilty, so heavy with guilt."

Third round: "What if I didn't have to feel this way? What if it's not my responsibility to take care of this person? That would feel really good; I would feel much lighter. I like that idea. What if feeling all this responsibility for other people was just something I learned from people who wanted me to take care of them? What if it was never true that I had to do that?"

Fourth round: "I wonder if it's possible for me to let go of believing that it's my job to take care of others. What if taking care of myself first didn't mean I was selfish? What if I didn't have to put my own needs last in order to be a good person? What if I could take care of myself and still be loved and safe?"

Fifth round: "I'm open to the possibility that I've been believing something that wasn't true for my whole life. I'm open to the possibility that it's not my responsibility to take care of others; it's not my job to make everyone else happy at my own expense. It feels good to think that. It makes sense. We all come from the same Source, so we all must have the same ability to find happiness. What if, by doing this for them, I'm preventing them from finding it themselves?"

Sixth round: "I'm willing to take a step back and allow others to take care of themselves. I'm willing to get out of the way and let God take care of them. I now see that I don't need to feel bad about putting my own needs first. I now see that I don't have to feel any guilt about this. The weight of the world is not on my shoulders. Maybe it once was, but it doesn't have to be anymore."

Seventh round: "I choose to let go of this guilt now. I choose to let go of feeling responsible for this person. I once believed it was my job to keep them happy/healthy/safe, but now I see that that is not true. It's based on a belief I adopted long ago, and I now know that it was false! I choose to erase the belief that has caused me to feel all this guilt. It was never my job to put this person's needs before my own. It was not my responsibility. I now choose to release this overwhelming feeling of responsibility and guilt. I release it now, and I am free."

My Story

Lines from my journal in 2002. I had left Kurt physically but realized he still had control over me psychologically and emotionally:

"He acted nice again yesterday—to get Luke for five days. I fell for it again. He would have accepted less. But I couldn't go through with it. So how do I imagine being able to leave him altogether?

Is this a test for me—to finally put my needs before his? Obviously still hard for me. But maybe that's what I have to learn. To see him unhappy and know that it's my fault. But that's just it. It wouldn't be. It's always up to him. He's always had the choice. He chooses to blame me for everything. I've got to be stronger in rejecting that blame. It's not my fault that he's unhappy. I've felt guilty since I left him. That's the power he's got over me. I'll never free myself from the past till I release that guilt. Till I do what I want to do, regardless of how it makes him feel."

The real test came not long after. I felt my higher self clearly telling me it was time to move back to Canada. This would mean putting thousands of miles between Kurt and our son, who was only three when this started. I had been battling guilt about separating them even just for a few days. How was I going to manage this?

The Universe gave me what I needed in order to grow. Judgment came from all sides. "A boy needs his father" was the current popular belief. Friends, so-called experts, and of course Kurt's family all judged me as selfish for wanting to move away. Kurt accused me in affidavits of doing it out of jealousy, because our son loved him more than me. To those who did not know me, this was a plausible scenario. The onus was on me to prove him wrong.

If the call to move back to my home country had been coming from anywhere other than my highest self, I'd have surely backed down. It was so hard to make people understand my motivation without being labeled as selfish or crazy. I couldn't tell the courts that I felt God was telling me to move to Canada (although that was the truth). They'd have taken my boy away from me in a heartbeat.

My role in my family of origin was caregiver. I felt responsible for the well-being and happiness of others, whether physically or emotionally, in different ways. But the one thing that was common to all of those relationships was that my needs came second to theirs. That was what I had been taught. That was what I believed. That was what I attracted.

I lived with that belief for so many years that it became my normal. Occasionally, I would notice a mild sense of frustration, but for the most part, I felt comfortable in my caregiver role. And that meant that it was my job to ensure that Kurt was happy, even if I had to sacrifice my happiness to achieve that. I was so well practiced in this for years that I didn't even notice when I was unhappy. I had learned to disconnect from my feelings so that I could continue taking care of others.

But now life was offering me the opportunity to break free from that prison. Hitting rock bottom had given me the courage to leave my marriage, but moving back to Canada was harder to justify to myself. Of course, there were some practical reasons, but the truth was I just wanted to go home, and as imperfect as it was, I wanted my boy to know his Canadian family. This longing had been in my heart since before Kurt and I even got together. Now it was making itself heard.

It was time to put my needs before his, and that threw my whole system into chaos. Part of me knew that this was what I had to do to be true to myself, and another part screamed, "Danger!" The last thing a people pleaser wants is to be judged as selfish. That's the power that others have over us. We'd rather sacrifice our own health and happiness than be considered selfish.

But what do we do when the still, small voice in our heart is telling us to do something that others will see as selfish? We make a choice. And I made mine.

Whether I won custody and permission to move back to Canada with my son or not was in God's hands. If I was meant to go, I would win. And then one day, in meditation, I realized something that made it possible for me to break free from all of that conditioning and judgment.

What I understood was God loves every single one of us equally, so how could it be that by following that voice, I could be hurting someone? God would never want that! And it dawned on me that as long as I was being true to myself, whatever I did would be for the highest good of anyone else involved.

That meant that this experience was exactly what Kurt needed for his highest good. It was an opportunity for his own healing and spiritual growth. Did that mean he grasped the lesson and did the work? I'll likely never know. But that's not mine to control. All I can do is trust that when I follow my own inner guidance, it will not be harmful to others. They may not like it, but in the wider scheme of things, it's just what they need.

So, I prayed for Kurt to see what Spirit wanted him to see, to learn what Spirit wanted him to learn through this painful experience. And I stepped out of the prison of guilt for doing what made me—and my son—happy. I'm not responsible for Kurt's happiness. I'm only responsible for my own.

I'll be honest. It's not like I never felt any twinge of guilt again, but I had freed myself enough to follow the path God wanted for me and move back to Canada, and I have not regretted it for a moment.

What's Mine? What's Yours?

The law of attraction approach to any given situation means always looking within to see what attracted it to you. There is no person or situation that you will experience that does not have its root within your being. Something had to have attracted it.

If you absolutely cannot imagine what it could be, meditation is necessary. Meditation will help you to see what aspects of your personality or memories you have been keeping hidden in your subconscious mind.

When you find the connection, often the current situation will resolve itself—seemingly miraculously! Other times, action on your part may be necessary. The action called for is usually the response that you needed to have in the original situation (that created this pattern) but for some reason were not able to. This can be speaking up about something, allowing yourself to cry, or just learning to let go of something or someone.

By approaching your life in this way, you will never be stuck in the thankless and fruitless role of trying to change somebody else. You will see that every experience you attract into your life is there as a lesson, to help you move forward on your spiritual journey. By looking within rather than pointing the finger of blame onto others, you will more easily learn what you need to in order to free yourself from the current pattern and move one step closer to inner freedom. As an added bonus, because of this approach, your relationships will be more harmonious!

By the same token, you will more easily be able to detach yourself from the moods and dramas of others, knowing that they are, in fact, just, projecting their buried issues onto you. People will try to tell you that they are upset because of something you did or said, but the truth is that they either attracted or interpreted your behaviour that way because of their own past patterns.

If you can look within and see that your behaviour was unfair or hurtful, of course you can apologize. But if you are involved with someone who always seems to be getting offended even by harmless comments you make, then you can stop trying to stand on your head to please them. Their issue is not with you. You can have a clear conscience as you gently suggest to this person that they learn to meditate, visit a therapist, or find some other way of uncovering what it is in them that is attracting this feeling of being hurt/offended all the time.

It is in their power and theirs alone to change that. Each of us can take responsibility not only for how we feel or react to situations but also for what situations in our lives come up and repeat themselves. Shining light on our inner lives is the best way to assure a harmonious and peaceful external experience.

ANGER

We learn to fear our own anger, not only because
it brings about the disapproval of others, but also
because it signals the necessity for change.
—Harriet Lerner

Congratulations! If you are reading this, it means you did not try to skip the chapter on anger!

Anger is a tricky subject. All of us have some anger inside us, but few of us are aware of it. Unless you've never been mistreated in your life or experienced grief of any kind, trust me, there's some anger in there. Why is it so hard for us to admit to this? Because here in the West, we live in a society that frowns upon expression of strong emotions. Many of us have parents or grandparents who practiced the art of "never let your feelings show." We equate anger with ugliness and violence and do our best to pretend it's not there. But it doesn't go away just because we won't look at it.

Some people who are in cruel or abusive relationships learn to suppress their anger so well that anyone who knows them would say they are sweet as honey and kind to everyone. The kindness is real. I'm convinced of that. But so is the justified anger that's being suppressed, and until it is acknowledged, self-damaging behaviors (read: addictions) are usually the way we keep it from surfacing.

People are often afraid of their anger. They are afraid that it will consume them and turn them into angry people. They are afraid that it will be too painful to let it come to the surface. They are afraid that their anger might make the situation worse. And I can't promise that none of these things will happen, but if you continue on your journey and don't stop halfway, they will all be temporary phases on the way to wholeness and healing.

There are others who do express their anger. They spend their lives getting angry at everyone for everything—their boss, other drivers, the government. It can feel toxic to be around them. These are the people who get sent to anger-management classes. Anger management is learning better coping strategies for dealing with your anger when it erupts, so that you can minimize the damage. That's certainly not a bad idea, and I'm sure it has helped many people.

The problem, however, is that even if we learn some coping skills for the acute situation, we will never be able to escape the pattern until we stop running from the real reason for our anger. If we get to the root of our anger, we can free ourselves from it entirely, so anger management would no longer be necessary. What I'd like to propose to you is *healing*, instead of just coping. Imagine one day being able to be free of that old rage that keeps surfacing and hurting the people you care about.

In my practice over the years, I've helped people get in touch with what they're really angry about. We can be totally convinced that the person we are really angry with is our boss, our spouse, our neighbor, or coworker. We have no problem expressing that anger to the stranger in the car that just cut us off or the cashier who accidentally punched in the wrong price, causing us to (gasp!) wait!

But when it comes to acknowledging where our anger originated, we back away in denial. How can we be angry with this person who did so much for us? Who is now so old and sickly? Who had such a hard childhood? Whom we are afraid of? Whose love and approval we so desperately long for? There are many reasons why we run from our anger, but none of them are healthy. I have watched many people find the courage to finally acknowledge who they are really angry with and why. In a safe environment, they give themselves permission to feel and explore this anger, and each time this happens, their load lightens.

Imagine being able to express your feelings of anger in a healthy way and no longer needing to run for the cookies, cigarettes, wine, and so on when you notice it surfacing. Imagine no longer going through your day feeling irritable and getting angry with people who really don't deserve it. Imagine feeling at peace with the world instead. It is possible, and you can begin right now.

Many people are afraid that if they give expression to their anger, they will not only become angry people but also attract negative energy. In fact, the opposite is true. By releasing the hidden anger, we clear our energy so that what we are sending out into the Universe is more positive, thus attracting more positive into our lives. Unexpressed anger weighs us down and sabotages our lives by attracting negative energy, even if we are not aware of its presence inside us. We think we're being positive, and we can't figure out why things keep going wrong. It's our suppressed anger! It often poisons not only our relationships but our bodies as well. Many illnesses can be healed or prevented by acknowledging our anger.

Every one of us is given a role to play in our family of origin. Because we grow up in this role, we are rarely aware of what it is or even of the fact that we have it. What you might notice instead is that you tend to behave in ways around your family or parents that you normally wouldn't, now that you're an adult. You might wonder why you do this and feel frustrated about it yet unable to do otherwise.

You've heard people say it before: "I'm a powerful CEO in my company, and yet when I get around my father, I feel like a bumbling idiot!" That's because you're unconsciously fulfilling your role. For a lot of us, that means denying our anger.

Exercise

Writing an anger letter is a good way of getting in touch with and releasing some of your hidden anger. This letter is not meant to be shown to anyone else. It is purely for your own inner cleansing.

You may want to begin by lighting a candle and saying a short prayer for healing. Have some tissues handy just in case. Take a few breaths to focus and begin.

Address the letter to whomever you wish, and then begin the first sentence with "I'm angry that ..." and complete the sentence. Write "I'm angry that ..." once again and complete the next sentence. Repeat this at least ten times or more, as needed. Even if you don't have an idea how the sentence will end, begin writing it and see what happens each time.

At the end, write, "I now give myself permission to feel this anger and to release it." When you are finished, don't reread the letter. Just tear it up or burn it, releasing your feelings of anger into the Universe, so they can be transformed.

My Story

One of my roles in my family was "the good girl." I was always upbeat, smiling, and laughing. Others, it seemed, were allowed to be in bad moods or get angry, but I never rocked the boat. If I did, I was judged harshly and usually punished with the silent treatment or worse. If I expressed anger, it was often met with even more anger or even rage. This was so hard to bear that I soon learned to keep my anger to myself. I swallowed the message that if I got angry, it would only make things worse. This lodged itself into my belief system and affected how I behaved in all my future relationships.

Needless to say, a person who is afraid to show anger is going to have a hard time creating a healthy relationship. People will do with you whatever you allow them to; push you as far as you'll let them. My conditioned behavior was to walk on eggshells, trying not to upset my partner. If they got angry with me, I felt afraid and guilty for whatever I'd done. I always blamed myself. I would adjust my behavior so as not to upset them this way again.

For example, in our early years together, Kurt would go on business trips regularly. When he was away, I would take the chance to spend some time with my friends (he didn't like them, so we didn't socialize together). One evening, when I was out late, he called home and didn't reach me (this was the pre–cell phone era). When we next spoke, he was very upset with me for this. I didn't question his anger. I didn't tell him that he had no reason to be angry with me. I didn't dare make things worse. True to my pattern, I decided to make sure that I was home by ten o'clock every night from then on, so he wouldn't be upset. I remember the look of disbelief on my friend's face one evening as I noticed the time and started to rush off from our lovely evening in a restaurant. When I explained to her that I had to get home for his call, she couldn't understand the urgency. I made excuses for him, but, of course, she was right. It would've been no big deal for him to call back later, but I was unable to see that. I'd upset him, and it was my job to make sure I didn't do it again.

I felt anger at times too, but the fear of making things worse led me to keeping it inside. And by that point in my life, I'd built my identity on the false notion that I simply did not get angry—because I was so nice. It affected my health and happiness in many negative ways until I finally started to acknowledge it. I ate to stuff down my anger. It didn't matter what as long as it was lots of it. And my skin suffered. Acne, abscesses, rashes were all trying to tell me to let it out, but I was too afraid of being punished if I did.

It's taken a lot of inner work for me to feel safe showing my anger. I had to learn that it is, in fact, a healthy emotion that signals to us that we are not being treated the way we deserve. Acknowledging my pent-up anger has freed me from continuing in that pattern and allowed me to find healthy ways to express my anger in current situations, so that it does not have to fester inside me or explode onto the wrong person anymore.

Today, if the above situation occurred, I would lovingly point out to my partner that he has no reason to be concerned if I am not available when he calls. I would recognize his insecurity as his issue and not take it on as mine. Reassuring him of my love, I would make it clear that I can't help him if he chooses to be angry about not reaching me when he calls and that it is his job to work on that. But of course, thanks to the law of attraction, my current partner is not someone who would even think of trying to control me in that way. As I have gradually learned that other people's reactions are their own issues and that I'm allowed to be angry too, I've changed the energy that I am sending out into the *Universe* and attracted someone who doesn't need me to be smiling all the time.

I now feel safe to express all my emotions in healthy ways. Who knew that I could be loved and loveable even when I feel angry? No more walking on eggshells!

EFT

Often we are so reluctant to allow our anger that even in meditation, we can't feel it. I have found that EFT works better in many cases for bringing up and clearing away our hidden anger.

Start with the karate chop point and say, "Even though I have anger inside me that I am afraid to feel, I deeply and completely love and accept myself." (Three times.)

Then tap through the points, saying:

"This anger. I feel angry. It's OK to feel anger. I'm angry about _____. I'm angry with _____. I'm allowed to be angry. It's safe for me to feel this anger." (Repeat any phrase that elicits a feeling, or add any that come to mind.)

When you start to feel the anger, make sure you keep tapping. Let it come to a climax and keep tapping as you really let it out—even if you have to scream or yell.

It's OK to yell things like "I hate you!" or "F— you!" while doing this; in fact, it's a great release of blocked energy if you can. If tears come, just keep tapping and let them flow.

Finally, once you've really connected with your anger, give yourself permission to release it. Tap through the points saying: "I now choose to release this anger from every cell in my body. I give myself permission to release this anger now, because I deserve to feel good. I acknowledge, accept, and release this anger. It's safe for me to feel my anger, and it's safe for me to let it go. I've been carrying it for long enough. Now I choose to be free of this anger."

When you're finished tapping, take a deep, slow breath and have a drink of water. You may want to have a nap or do a meditation to calm your energy.

Thought, Word, Deed

What you think, feel, say, and do are all forms of energy. If they are not in alignment with one another, the Universe will not be able to help you, as you will be giving it mixed messages. If you think you'd like to be wealthy but feel like you can't afford to eat at your favorite high-end restaurant, you are giving a mixed message. If you feel like you want to find your soul mate but say you love being single (to save face), you are sending a mixed message. If you go to the gym or diet regularly to feel better about yourself but feel guilty about eating and say that you are fat, you are sending a mixed message.

If something you want hasn't manifested, have a closer look at your thoughts, feelings, words, and actions on the subject. Make sure you are sending out one consistent message because it's all energy!

SELF-LOVE/SELF-ACCEPTANCE

All you need is love.
—John Lennon

John Lennon had it right. It was a profound, spiritual truth he was singing about back in the 1960s, but most people did not understand that at the time. With the Hollywood version of love dominating the media, it is not hard to see how cynics would take the powerful lyrics to this song and label them naive or utopian.

But when we come closer to understanding the true nature of love, including self-love, compassion, and divine love, it becomes more difficult to dismiss the claim that love is all you need. In my experience, love truly is the answer to all problems and challenges, and self-love is where it starts.

In my work over the past ten years, I have not come across a single person who had a healthy feeling of self-love or self-acceptance. None of us had perfect parents. Even if you had parents who were fair-tempered and respectful of you, it is incredibly difficult for any parent to completely avoid passing on feelings of unworthiness to their children on some level, if they feel unworthy themselves. As a parent, the best thing you can do for your child is to work on loving and accepting yourself. That is the best way I have found to be able to raise a confident and grounded child. Our children learn through example, so be an example of someone who loves and accepts themselves if you want your kids to do the same. Or at least be an example of someone who has made learning to love themselves a priority. It's OK for your kids to see you working at it. Modelling the courage, integrity, and faith that this path takes is an invaluable gift to your children for their own journeys.

So if your parents didn't love or accept themselves, they would not have been able to love and accept you the way you deserved to be. We are all beautiful, magnificent creations of the Universe, but with our upbringing, we are often convinced otherwise. We are told that we are too much of this and not enough of that. Our parents, teachers, and other adults around us project their feelings of inadequacy onto us, and as obedient children, we come to feel inadequate over time.

Sometimes the messages we get are far worse than being simply inadequate. Some of us have been told outright that we are worthless, ugly, lazy, useless, unwanted, or unloved. We've been blamed for other people's moods or misfortunes; scapegoated for things the adults in our lives did not want to see in themselves. Some parents have outright sabotaged their children's chances for happiness because of their unwillingness to do their own healing work. Perhaps they were not completely conscious of the damage they were doing, but somewhere deep inside, I think a part of us is aware of it when we avoid looking honestly at ourselves. And when we do that, those close to us suffer.

Not only those whose parents were overtly abusive suffer from feelings of self-rejection. If we allow ourselves to look deep enough inside, it seems to be there in all of us. Why look? Because remembering our perfection is why we're here. Because learning that you deserve to be loved just for showing up—without having to do or be anything for anyone—is an amazing feeling. Because if you avoid looking, you'll remain stuck in coping behaviors forever.

Some of us hide from our deep feelings of unworthiness by staying busy; others by stuffing them down with food. Sometimes it's shopping that distracts us from our self-rejection, or gambling, drinking, video games or drugs that numb us out so we don't have to feel it. No one is exempt. And sooner or later, we have to face how we've been taught to feel about ourselves if we want to be happy.

Here's the good news: if the people around you were not able to love you the way you were meant to be loved—cherished, adored, and made to feel special—you are not doomed to repeat that pattern for the rest of your life. You can begin by learning to love and accept yourself, and that will reflect in the experiences you draw to you in the outside world. If you are not feeling loving toward yourself, how can you attract a mate who will? If you don't respect yourself, how can you attract friends who do? It doesn't matter how long you've been unloving toward yourself. If you start to change your thoughts and behavior right now, others will see you differently, and your life will begin to change.

Many people settle for a lukewarm relationship rather than insisting on finding real love. They stay in the comfort zone of what is familiar, even if it leaves their hearts longing for more. It is scary to go beyond the boundaries of what you've known till now, but finding real love is why we are here. We are love, and as we experience life with wounded people, we gradually forget that. Our task is to get back to that place—to knowing that we can never be separated from love because it's who we are in our essence.

This is not easy at first, but it gets easier the more you work on it. And the sooner you start, the sooner your life will change.

For me, learning to love myself was intertwined with learning that God loves me. Sometimes it was easier to phrase it that way than to say, "I love myself," but it led to the same great feeling. It doesn't matter in the end how you say it. The only thing that matters is that you feel loved. It may take a while before you feel anything at all. You might feel sadness, anger, or frustration. These are all healthy reactions along your path of recognizing that you weren't loved as you deserved to be. Eventually, you will notice that your self-critical voice is getting quieter. As you practice more loving thoughts, they will come more naturally to you. You'll start noticing that the people in your life are treating you better, or new ones are entering who do. That's proof that you are really beginning to love yourself.

You can't trick the Universe. If you want to attract love, you've got to really love yourself first. A lot of people want to rush past the inevitable tears and pain as their hearts begin to open in places that have been long shut and just say, "I love myself!" without really feeling it. Then they wonder why nothing's changing in their relationships and perhaps decide that affirmations don't work.

To let real love in, we have to let some unpleasant stuff out. Resistant thoughts will come up. We have to look at them honestly before we can discard them. This takes courage, but it's absolutely worth it.

You are creating your external life with every thought you think. If you are not feeling deeply and completely loved, keep doing the work. In fact, even if you are, keep doing it because the experience of love can always go deeper. And you deserve that.

Exercise

Make a list of ten things you don't like about yourself.

Now make a list of ten things you do like about yourself.

Which list was easier to write? Why? Write down your answers. How easy is it for you to say positive things about yourself? How does it make you feel?

Why is self-love important in the working of the law of attraction? The degree to which you are able to love yourself determines how worthy you feel of receiving anything good from the Universe. Think of it this way: if you had a great gift to give away and you had to choose between a person you really liked and another who you did not think highly of, which one would you give the gift to?

Of course, the person you like, right? So now what if that person is you, and the gift is all the blessings of the Universe? As long as you persist in criticizing and rejecting yourself, you are keeping the door shut to all those blessings.

Some parts of ourselves are so hard for us to accept that we have relegated them into the darkness permanently. (Read more on this in chapter on projection.) If you want to truly learn to love yourself, you have to include *all* of yourself—even the parts you try to hide from the world. You hide them because you think they make you unlovable. This is typical for those of us who put on a smile even when we're feeling angry or sad. We think the world will reject us if we show our true feelings, so we pretend to be happy and bubbly instead. But that rejected part remains within us, sending out the message that we are unlovable and unworthy. So you remain that nice person who never seems to find the right partner. You're rejecting yourself and then wondering why others reject you as well! If you want to attract new and more loving experiences into your life, you've got to clear out *all* of the negative beliefs about yourself—even the hidden ones.

Practice focusing your attention on the things you like about yourself and add to that list as you grow in self-acceptance. And with the other list, practice seeing those things you don't like about yourself and loving yourself anyway.

For example, perhaps you wrote: I am always late.

Practice saying, "I am not punctual, and I am perfect just the way I am."

Perhaps you wrote: I get angry too easily.

Practice saying, "Even though I get angry easily, I love myself just the way I am."

Perhaps you wrote: I need to lose twenty pounds.

Practice saying, "I love my body just as it is, and I am lovingly taking good care of it."

A lot of people fear that by accepting themselves as they are, they are saying they don't want to change. That is not what self-love is about. You can still work on being more punctual, controlling your temper, or losing weight, but the key is to *love yourself first*. If you say you'll love and accept yourself after these things change, then you are offering yourself conditional love. And what if you don't ever lose those twenty pounds? Will you spend the rest of your life rejecting yourself?

If you do, you will be cutting yourself off from being in the flow. Your life will feel like a constant struggle. By beginning with self-love, you bring yourself into the flow, and there you receive all the support of the Universe in being your highest and best self. Instead of seeing your imperfections as things you need to fix in order to be worthy of love, focus on your spiritual growth and learn to love yourself, warts and all. Since your internal reality creates your external, others will see you as a loveable person as you learn to love yourself more.

My Story

Racism is an ugly thing. I often heard my parents and relatives speaking angrily about their experiences of it in Winnipeg. When I was three years old, we moved to a new suburb on the edge of town where many people had farms nearby. I was the only Indian girl in my class until grade ten, when one more brown-skinned girl joined our school.

I was called names and shoved against the lockers; my entire family was bullied and harassed constantly. Our fence often got kicked in, our front windows egged. "Pakis go home" was spray-painted on the fence regularly. We would paint over it, and within days, those hateful words would be back. We were made to feel unwelcome because we were different, but we couldn't help being different. So we were unwanted simply for being who we were.

I grew up feeling ashamed of my skin color; ashamed to be who I was. I remember sitting sadly in front of my mirror as a ten-year-old child and wishing that I had white skin so that I could be like the others. I recall a teacher asking each child in grade three what they'd had for dinner the night before. As we went around the circle, all I remember is the feeling of panic as my turn approached. The kids were all saying things like hamburgers or pizza. I'd had curried chicken and rice, one of our weekly staples. The year was 1973. Back then, curry wasn't the popular, well-loved dish it is today. Again I was going to be different. Again I risked being ridiculed, as I imagined the other kids scrunching their noses at me and asking, "What's that?"

So when my turn came, I quietly lied. "Hamburgers," I mumbled. Phew! They bought it, and it was now the next person's turn. I'd stayed safe by pretending to be someone I was not. This would, unfortunately, become a habit.

Growing up in the last days of the British Empire, having dark skin was still very much a disadvantage. The darker your skin, the lower your value as a human being. That's what the British taught their colonies. My father, growing up in colonial Trinidad and Tobago, never managed to move past that belief and the pain it caused.

He inevitably passed that pain down to his children, as is always the case with unresolved feelings. It's hard to heal from inherited pain, because you can't recall a time when it wasn't there. It can be scary to let it go, not knowing what will fill the space it occupied. Sometimes we identify ourselves by that inherited pain, or we feel too guilty to let it go because it caused our parents so much suffering. Sometimes we hold a hidden belief that it is the only thing keeping us connected to our parents. It was not an easy process or a quick one, but after several years of inner work, I have finally come to a place where I can feel proud of my skin color and my Indian heritage.

Along my healing journey and in working with my clients, I realized something very interesting. I, by no means, wish to belittle the traumatic effect of racism, but the feelings of low self-worth that I struggled with seemed to be present in my clients too, who were mostly Caucasian. Whether it stemmed from having alcoholic parents or some form of abuse; whether they were discriminated against for being overweight or poor; whether they were shunned for having a parent who either left or died early; or they were teased for being too good or not very bright at school, they were all dealing with a deep, haunting feeling of not being good enough, just like me. I saw that everyone's parents had managed to pass on some form of unresolved pain and unworthiness, not just mine. This was eye-opening and so helpful in letting go of seeing myself as a victim. Everyone's dealing with something. And only love can heal us.

Of course, feeling unworthy made it impossible to attract a partner who truly loved me, as long as I was unaware. How could I attract love when I didn't love myself? The man I married reflected back to me my own self-rejection and sense of unworthiness. Nothing I did was right. I unconsciously gave him the power to tell me what I was worth. We don't realize when we're doing this if it's our pattern; it's the only way of being that we know. If I behaved in the ways he wanted me to, I got his approval. My sense of self-worth was so low (although you wouldn't have known it to see me; I was a well-trained pretender) that I was dependent on his approval. This is how I gave him my power. And of course, he was a blond, green-eyed German man, the type of person I'd been programmed to believe was superior to me.

Thanks to my meditation practice and rebirthing therapy, this began to change very gradually after the birth of our son. I'd had a hard time standing up for myself when it was just about me, but when it came to our son, I started finding courage I didn't know was there.

I recall a pivotal moment when I showed Kurt two sets of pajamas I'd bought for our eight-month-old son. Without realizing it, I'd slipped into the habit of not purchasing anything unless he was there to give his approval. I guess it happened because the few times I did, he didn't like what I chose, so I began to mistrust my ability to make good choices. It seemed safer to just let him make the decisions. That way, I didn't risk losing his approval. As my self-esteem began to grow, so did my faith in myself. I was starting to realize that his disapproval of whatever I bought had more to do with maintaining his power than with my supposed lack of taste. It was just another way of making me feel inadequate, and I was ready to challenge it.

So on this day, I dared bring home these baby clothes I'd purchased without his consent, and when I showed them to him, he was true to form.

"They're ugly. Take them back," he said dismissively, barely looking up from the television. And normally I would've done just that. But this time I said no. My spiritual practice was helping me to feel stronger and more confident. As I opened up to feeling God's love for me, I became less dependent on his. I kept the pajamas and dressed our son in them regularly. Small steps toward freedom.

Kurt didn't like the changes he saw in me. One day, he even said, "Your therapy is making you egotistic." What it was really doing was making me aware of my own needs for the first time in my life. His criticism hurt, because it was something I was really uncomfortable with being called. I had a belief that if I didn't do what others wanted me to, I was being selfish. My therapist helped me to see that he was actually a great teacher for me. He was saying exactly what I needed to hear in order to overcome this false belief, and that I did.

I was learning that my needs mattered too. I was learning that my opinions count. I was learning to treat myself with the love and respect I'd always longed for from others. If it seemed a little selfish of me to start putting my needs first now and then, so be it. I hoped that he would be able to adjust to the new me, but he couldn't. I was hoping that we could work through this and grow together. He was as much stuck in his patterns as I was in mine. I pleaded with him to see a therapist as well, but he wouldn't. I left him about a month after the pajama incident. My self-esteem had been severely damaged in our years together, but I was on my way back up. I knew I deserved to be treated better than this. I knew that one day the Universe would send me a loving partner who respected and cherished me. But it would never happen as long as I continued to accept being treated like a second-class citizen in my own home.

It took me about five or six years of working with my meditations and affirmations before the day came when I finally felt the words "I love myself just the way I am" reach my heart. I cried many tears before that day and even more on that day. It felt great to have rewired my brain and healed my heart to the point that I really and truly loved myself.

The Universe confirmed this change in my energy by sending me a loving partner. Seven more years passed before Jon entered my life. I needed that time to really change how I saw myself so that I could finally be in a healthy relationship. His behavior toward me is a reflection of all the new beliefs that I have established, and that feels wonderful! He's the polar opposite of the kind of man I used to attract; he makes me feel special, loved, and like I matter.

I am certain that if I had not stayed on this healing path of learning to love and accept myself, I would never have met Jon. In fact, I did meet kind and thoughtful men in the past, but my feelings of not being worthy caused me to either drive them away or run away myself.

Another gift I have found by learning to love myself is a freedom within my relationship that I never had before. I am no longer the people-pleasing girl who accepted being treated badly because she so desperately needed to be loved. I'm still working on being true to myself—not pretending to be happy when I'm not. Not pretending—period. The amazing thing is that instead of feeling like I have to have my guard up with my partner in case he tries to have power over me like in my past, Jon actually encourages and supports me in being true to myself. He's not at all interested in having power over me. Wow! What a welcome change!

With a loving partner by my side today, I am learning to voice my true thoughts, feelings, and needs without fear of angering him or losing his love, because I feel secure in the knowledge that I am loved. I am loved simply for being here and just as I am, by the Source that created me, the essence of which lives inside me and is pure and divine. Whenever I forget that, all I have to do is sit still and breathe, and I am reminded again and again of just how loveable and beautiful I am. And on a day when this is challenging, I now have a loving partner who happily reminds me!

Meditate on Self-Love

Sit quietly or lie down. Start to notice your breath. Just focus on your breathing for two or three minutes. Then shift your attention to your heart and feel a connection with your heart. Once you feel the connection, say (in your mind) the following affirmations:

"I am perfect just the way I am. I love and accept myself just as I am. I love my body just as it is, and I honor myself by taking good care of it."

Competition

Ego sees itself as separate from others and most often also in competition with them. Our society promotes competition, which begins in the very first days of school, if not sooner. A question is asked, and the child with the right answer receives praise. The others want praise as well, so they determine to get the next answer right. If they do, they're better than the others. If they don't, they feel less valuable, and the next step is to find somewhere where they can prove themselves and receive the coveted attention that we all instinctively crave.

Most people carry this attitude of competition into their adult lives, which traps them into thought patterns of judging and criticizing not only others but themselves as well. Our attitudes toward our bodies are a good example of how competitive thinking pervades our thoughts and becomes so habitual that we don't even notice that we are having them. As a society, women in particular are conditioned to feel that our bodies should be as slim as they were when we were twenty years old, even when we are fifty. And heaven help those who weren't even slim at twenty! With that message coming at us through magazines, movies, and commercials on a daily basis, many of us go around with a constant internal dialogue of comparing our bodies to everyone we encounter on any given day.

The way out of this is to practice self love and self acceptance.

9

EXPECTATIONS AND SELF-SABOTAGE

Now faith is the substance of things hoped
for, the evidence of things not seen.
—Hebrews 11:1

The beliefs that we have about ourselves and the world are what create our experience of reality. As discussed in earlier chapters, our external lives are simply reflections of our internal ones. What we believe becomes what we expect, and what we expect is what we get.

Sometimes our hidden beliefs lead us to expect bad things to happen, otherwise known as disaster thinking. This means as soon as things seem to be going well for you in one way or another, you start to be on the alert. Not used to the idea that happiness could last, you are expecting it to end, and you need to keep on your toes to protect yourself from being hurt when it does. You never let your guard down. You did that once, and look what happened.

Disaster thinking creates worst-case scenarios in our heads and haunts us with them.

Do you see images of people you love getting hurt when you close your eyes? Do you have a deep-seated feeling that happiness can't last? Are you always waiting for the other shoe to drop? The origins for this kind of thinking can vary widely, but the result is the same. We create the expectation that we will be disappointed, unhappy, and hurt.

Through my years of meditating and studying scriptures of various religious traditions, I am convinced that the higher intelligence in the Universe truly supports us in enjoying our lives. We are meant to be happy. Take that in: we are meant to be happy! Sadly, in my work with clients, I've discovered that most people don't believe that. Most people, at least here in the West, seem to accept the idea that life is meant to be a struggle and that even if happiness comes our way, disappointment won't be far behind. This fundamental distrust in the Universe is the cause for so much suffering and unhappiness. It's unnecessary, and you can change it—starting now.

Your thoughts create your reality, and you create your thoughts. You weren't always aware that you were doing so, but now that you are, you have the power to change them! Let's take a common example. Look at your parents. If they reached a certain level of prosperity, happiness, or health, you likely have a subconscious limitation that will not allow you to surpass them. This may not be true in every area of your life, but if there's one you find yourself struggling with repeatedly, you could be sabotaging yourself out of what I call "invisible loyalty."

So even though you may manage to secure a well-paying job, you either can't enjoy the money or you make bad investments—anything to keep you from being happier than your parents were. I call it invisible loyalty because we are usually blind to the fact that our suffering is connected to the ways we perceive our parents to have suffered. Out of a sense of loyalty that we are unaware of, we hold ourselves back from being richer, healthier, or happier than our parents. Of course, it's not always this direct. You may surpass your parents financially but sabotage your happiness in the area of love and relationships. Or you may surpass your parents in both of those areas, only to even it out with health problems. The aim of the invisible loyalty is to keep you from "betraying" your parents by suffering less than they did.

Or maybe you experienced trauma in your early years, and that resulted in a belief that happiness can't last. Then even if you find happiness in every area of your life, you will chase it away somehow, to fulfill your expectation that life is painful and disappointing. Have you ever accused yourself of screwing things up all the time? Go easy on yourself.

People are largely unaware when they are sabotaging their lives. We tend to feel more like these things are just happening to us because we don't understand the power of our thoughts.

If you believe that life is a struggle, every time things get easier for you, you'll unconsciously find a way to make it difficult again. If you watched your parents go through an ugly divorce—or stay in an unhappy marriage—you are likely carrying some guilt. No matter what kind of partner you manage to attract into your life, unless you do some inner work to move beyond the limits of your parents, your invisible loyalty will make sure that you don't surpass the level of happiness you witnessed in them. There can certainly be other influences besides our parents, but they are often the strongest factors in determining what level of happiness we expect to have in our lives.

As long as you expect a hard life, the Universe will grant you one. We need to start believing that good things can come into our lives easily and stay. Otherwise we will chase away every blessing that comes to us. Expect to be treated with love and respect. Expect to live in prosperity and comfort. Expect today to be a wonderful day. Expect happiness and love to last.

Since your patterns of expecting disaster are hidden in your subconscious mind, once again, meditation is the key to uncovering them so that you can create new and positive ones.

It can be hard to accept that we are actually sending out messages that invite us to be hurt, especially because in our minds we might think we are saying all the right things: "I want a man who loves me! When is it going to be my turn to feel special? I'm tired of being treated this way!"

But it's the subconscious thoughts, the ones in the dark, which are more powerful in creating our lives. *Why would anyone love me? If they really knew me, they'd leave me. Intimate relationships terrify me.*

No matter what you think you might be expecting, I encourage you to use meditation to help you see what's going on beneath the surface.

Based on what you experienced in your past, how do you really expect your life to unfold? Can you actually imagine being treated like a queen, or does it make you uncomfortable? Can you imagine a relationship that lasts forever, or does it scare you? How about being wealthy? Healthy? Truly happy?

Unless you clear away old expectations and choose healthier ones to replace them, you will continue to repeat the old patterns. By learning to expect love instead of heartache, joy instead of disappointment, being treated like a queen rather than a second-class citizen, that is exactly what I got.

Meditate

Sit quietly or lie down. Start to notice your breath. Just focus on your breathing for two or three minutes. You can count from one to five over and over to keep your attention on your breath. Now allow your inner wisdom to show you what area of your life you have been sabotaging. Keep breathing and open yourself to being shown why. Everything you need to know is inside you. Resist the temptation to think and just breathe and observe instead. Once you've received some clarity, end your meditation with the following affirmations: "I let go of expecting to be hurt. That was the past. I now expect to be happy and loved. I am happy and loved!"

My Story

Like so many others, I experienced disappointment as a child. I never really felt loved for who I was; love was conditional. There were certainly happy times, but they never seemed to last. Because of the mood swings of some of my family members, I felt like I was always waiting for a bomb to go off, and it was usually when I least expected it.

Having my mother become ill and gradually slip away in my teen years added powerfully to the feeling that happiness could not last.

Looking back, I realize that every romantic relationship I was in was doomed from the start. My belief that love and happiness could not last became my expectation. It was so subtly there inside me that I never saw it. I only see now that it was there because it's finally gone. We often only notice something once it's gone, and in this case, that's a good thing.

It was like a little voice inside me was saying, "Of course, you knew this had to happen," every time one of my relationships came to a heartbreaking end. Even during the relationship, I would find ways to sabotage the harmony if it went on for too long, because on some level, it made me uncomfortable. I didn't trust it. I would start arguments or make accusations of my partner, without any awareness that I was causing the very pain and drama that I felt I was the victim of. How could I have known that I was sabotaging my happiness through my own expectations?

Of course, it's a vicious cycle because if you expect something so much that you can't really even imagine anything else, it will manifest in your life. It has to. So I went through life longing for love and searching for happiness but expecting pain and disappointment. The results were exhausting and heartbreaking.

One incident I recall was within my first months with Kurt. I was in the process of building up a clientele for my language school, so I wasn't earning much money yet. He had an old yellow rain jacket with black marks on it from oil or dirt, and he commented that he needed to get a new one. He had also remarked that I needed one, because we spent a lot of time walking outside.

One day he came home with a shopping bag and seemed excited. I greeted him, anxious to see what he'd bought. As he pulled a shiny new green rain jacket out of the bag, I gasped like a little girl getting a surprise. That's what I thought was happening as he held it up and asked me, "What do you think?"

"I think it's really nice!" I exclaimed. But my joy was short-lived. As I watched him pull it over his head, I was a little confused for a second. Then he went to the cupboard and pulled out the old, yellow, stained jacket. Handing it to me with a smile, he said, "And you can have this one!"

My heart sank all the way into my belly, and I didn't say a word. A voice in my head was saying, "What else did you expect? Idiot! Of course you don't get the new one! How ridiculous of you to even think so! Don't dare show that you even had that thought or he'll probably laugh at you. How embarrassing! Quick—smile and pretend you're happy! Say thank you and mean it. You're lucky after all. Who do you think you are to expect the new jacket anyway?"

I was crestfallen. As much as I wanted to think that I'd found my prince, the reality was I was in a two-tiered relationship. I had felt like a second-class citizen in my family, so of course, how could it be any different now? Hand-me-downs were the norm. My older sister logically got the new clothes, then the second oldest, and then me. That in itself wouldn't have to be the end of the world, but there were many other ways in which I got the message that I was somehow worth less than others in the family.

There were lots of baby photos of my two older sisters but none of me. I'm not exaggerating. I was thirty years old, visiting my aunt in Trinidad, when I saw a photo of myself as a baby for the first time. I used to joke as a teenager that I must've been adopted, but that was just my way of covering up the confusion and sadness. No explanation was ever offered, so I just assumed that I was simply not as important as my siblings.

Also, as the third girl in an Indian family, if there was ever a serious discussion or a decision to be made, my oldest sister's opinion would be asked, occasionally my next older sister, but never mine. I sat at the table with everyone else, but my opinion was of no value. I often felt invisible.

After years of meditating and shedding light on my beliefs, I managed to uncover these memories and work on healing the feeling of being less than. I learned that I am someone valuable and dared to expect to be treated that way. I let go of expecting to be disappointed and hurt and chose to believe that happiness and love last and that I deserve both. I even decided not to settle for anything less than a partner who made me feel special and treated me like a queen! What a long shot that seemed at the time!

With persistence and lots of inner work, I gradually got myself to a place where I was able to manifest exactly that. Not only does Jon treat me like a queen, but without any prompting on my part, he even calls me his queen! Isn't the Universe amazing? It's always listening and responding to our expectations.

Making a Difference

I have heard criticisms of enlightened teachers, like Eckhart Tolle, claiming that his teachings are useless in solving the problems of the real world. The tone is often a little self-righteous: "What about getting your hands dirty, Mr. Tolle, and coming down to feed the starving children with us instead of spouting all this airy-fairy advice?"

When I hear these things, I know that there is no point engaging in a conversation with this person. They are simply not yet at the level of awareness that would help them see how incredibly powerful the work of spiritual masters like Eckhart is in changing the world. When you grasp that everything has to exist first on the energy level before it can manifest in the physical world, you see how futile it is to simply hand out food. I'm not saying that it isn't a good thing to do. For those whose heart chakra is awakening, acts of charity are normal expressions of the awareness that we are all connected. It's an important stage to go through in our spiritual development, but as history shows us, it is not creating permanent change. That's why many people involved in any kind of struggle against social injustice become frustrated, disillusioned, and exhausted.

On the physical level, they are trying to change something that they unconsciously continue to create through their limited thinking.

I worked in inner-city ministry for several years and witnessed the kind of scarcity thinking that prevails there. The church I was working with was facing yearly cuts in funding and wondering whether they would even survive another year. There was a lot of talk of having to cut down here and spend less there. Fear-based thinking was the norm.

At a strategic-planning meeting, we were all asked what our vision for the ministry was. I shared that my vision was one of abundance, where everyone who came would have enough to satisfy their hunger, and we wouldn't have to limit what we could give out.

Not long after that, I took over the position of running the ministry. We soon managed to arrange for daily donations of bread and desserts from a nearby supermarket and a local bakery, which allowed us not only to serve sandwiches and delicious desserts to our guests but also to supply many of them with loaves and muffins to take home! We attracted generous volunteers, who showed up with soup, fruit, and many other treats.

We ended that first year with a surplus in our budget of $5,000. Never before had that been the case! The explanation of the board was that donations had been higher than usual that year … why? Because we visualized abundance. We talked abundance, we practiced abundance (generosity), and we believed in abundance.

If it can happen in an inner-city ministry of a church whose financial support was being reduced every year, it can happen anywhere. Everything starts as a thought, which is energy. It becomes words, which are energy. Then it manifests into form, which is also energy. Working to change something on the physical level without changing the energy that creates it can bring about temporary change, but your thought patterns will inevitably keep you going in circles. Starting with shifting your energy, which means doing the inner work first, is the only way to allow for true transformation.

PATIENCE

Infinite patience brings immediate results.
—A Course in Miracles

I can't even begin to tell you how important this one is. Without patience, the law of attraction simply cannot work in your life. What is patience? I think it is more than the ability to wait. In fact, I think patience and faith are very close in meaning. Faith means trusting that everything is unfolding as it should. Patience is just the same as that, with the added clause … according to divine timing.

We live in a society of immediate gratification; we want everything, and we want it fast! I am often amused when people are looking something up on their computers and get fidgety if they have to wait more than five seconds for it to load. Often you'll hear them grumbling about how slow it is and clicking repeatedly on their mouse, as if that is going to make it faster.

Gandhi once said that there is more to progress than just making things faster. Unfortunately, we didn't quite get that. If we are impatient by our nature, perhaps we would do better to cultivate an attitude of patience, rather than speeding up everything to accommodate our lack thereof. In our quest for speed, we miss out on the opportunity for spiritual growth that comes with learning the art of patience.

In my experience, the reward for learning patience is becoming a patient person. That may not sound like much, but when it comes to the law of attraction, it's invaluable.

When you ask for something, sometimes it can appear right away. However, some requests take longer to manifest than others, depending on how much resistance we have on the subject.

We've already talked about the importance of being able to receive. It's a challenge to be receptive to the things we desire, and even more challenging to stay receptive when, after a while, nothing external has manifested. This is a huge problem, because even if you are open to begin with, the moment you start to ask, "When is it coming?" you close yourself off from receiving again.

Becoming impatient implies doubt—a lack of faith as it were. If we can fully trust that our intentions will manifest when the time is right, then we don't need to ask when it's coming or why it's not here yet. Both of those imply a lack of faith. All we need to do is stay open to the belief that it is on its way and enjoy the present moment.

Often we get so caught up in the attitude of impatient waiting that we lose the potential joy of the present moment. Our thoughts and feelings are energy, and they are attracting like energies into our lives, so we block ourselves from receiving what we want if we spend the present moment in impatient dissatisfaction. In fact, if like attracts like and your goal is to be happy, then the most powerful thing you can do to manifest your desires is to be happy without them! If you can create the feeling of happiness that you would have once your desire was fulfilled— and feel it now—you will be helping the Universe to bring it to you. Being able to wait in faith while the Universe aligns itself so that your desires can manifest is a key to cocreating your life.

We in the West have a particularly hard time with this, because we are taught that we need to do something if we want to achieve anything. Having enough faith to simply wait and trust is challenging enough for most of us, but in addition, we often have to bear the ridicule and judgment of those around us. The need to be *doing something* comes from ego, which wants to feel like it's still in control. But often the very things that the Universe needs to rearrange in order to be able to fulfill your wishes are within you, and this work can only be done if we are willing to slow down and rest.

The metaphor of the caterpillar cocooning has been used so often because it is one of nature's most powerful examples of the importance of waiting. What would happen to the caterpillar if we decided we needed to open up the cocoon earlier to speed up the process? What would happen to the seedling if we tugged on it to help it grow? How many possibilities are we missing out on in our lives because we simply don't have the patience and faith to wait it out?

Jesus told us, "...What things soever ye desire, when ye pray, believe that ye receive them, and ye shall have them." (Mark 11:24). If you believe you have received it, then you will feel happy now. That's how you come into vibrational alignment with what you want, which allows you to receive it. If you understand the law of attraction, then you know that what you've asked for will come—in divine timing. Everything happens at the right time, and when we try to rush things, we do more damage than good.

So instead of trying to speed things up, we can cultivate patience so that we can wait in peace. Meditation is one of the best ways I know to practice patience.

Exercise

Take some time to reflect on the following. How do you react when ...

1. You are sitting at a red light that is taking a long time to change.
2. You are in line at the grocery store, and the person in front of you is very slow.
3. You are surfing the internet, and it's taking longer than usual to load.

If you notice that you become impatient in any of these scenarios, then try this simple exercise. As you are waiting, start to count your breaths. Count from one to ten and then start at one again. This will bring you into the present moment, which has the automatic effect of making you feel calmer. Of course, you can apply this approach to any situation where you notice yourself becoming impatient. Practicing patience with little things helps cultivate patience for big things as well.

Whether you get frustrated or not, the light isn't going to turn green until it's time. You can't change that, but you can change how you feel while you are waiting. The quote at the beginning of this chapter says, "Infinite patience brings immediate results." The immediate result is that you are at peace the moment you choose to practice patience. You don't have to wait to make that choice. That's what you can do now, and if you do, what you're waiting for will flow more easily to you.

My Story

After I filed for divorce, the stuff hit the fan, as you can imagine. Kurt's pride was hurt, and now that it was clear that there would be no reconciliation, there was no holding back on the hostility. He became violent in his whole demeanor and physically assaulted me one day as our three-year-old son sat in the car and watched, bawling.

I didn't understand narcissism at the time, but years later, I recognized his behavior in the descriptions I read, both during our marriage and after. It helped me understand his anger about the fact that I'd left him. How dare I leave such a perfect man? It seemed from the moment I filed for divorce, his sole focus was to make me miserable in whatever way he could, and he didn't mind using our son to get there.

Luke developed a persistent dry cough that lasted for about six months, and he also began nervously rubbing his fingers together, so much that he developed eczema on his hands. The doctor tried several different remedies but to no avail. When we were in Winnipeg a few months later, I noticed how much happier and more confident Luke was. There were digestive issues as well before our trip, but all of these symptoms disappeared after we'd been in Winnipeg for just a week. It was so wonderful to see my baby feeling better and happier than he'd been in so long. When the day came to fly back to Germany, I felt immobilized. My logical side said we had to go back, but it was drowned out by the cries of my heart.

How could I take my child, now thriving and among family, back to an environment where I was all but certain his suffering would return? His father spoke ill about me in front of Luke regularly and refused to let him call me when he missed me, as I later learned, which resulted in fits of anger and tears after each weekend with his dad. He was not physically violent with him (as far as I know), but he played mind games with him.

On top of all this, I feared for my safety as well as Luke's. Kurt seemed to have become obsessed with the idea of making me suffer, and there was no telling where his limits were. He had applied for sole custody and was trying to convince social workers and the courts that I was mentally unfit to parent our son. The man I once trusted and loved had turned into my worst enemy, and I was afraid.

He had the support of his whole family, who'd all turned on me, except for one aunt (whom I will never forget). He had the money, the language, and the home advantage.

I felt completely alone. It was in this life phase that I made meditation a daily practice, simply to stay functional for my son and to keep the fear under control. It worked.

Seeing Luke's improvement, coupled with my father's failing health, every cell in my body was resisting getting on that flight back to the nightmare that my life in Germany had become. Through meditation, the message had come several times that we were meant to move back to Canada, and I trusted that inner voice. So I found the courage to call up Luke's father the next day, hoping for a miracle.

Kurt reacted with rage. Perhaps part of it was truly about love for his son, but I knew that a bigger part of it was that he had had control of me for years, and he was not about to let it go that easily. He flew to Canada and took me to court. I was ordered to go back to Germany and let the courts there decide. Until a custody decision was made, I was not allowed to leave the country with our son, unless Kurt gave me permission. He was in his element. Power was what he wanted.

About a year later, as the hearings continued to be delayed and Kurt continued to put up roadblocks, I got the news that my father had had a heart attack, back in Canada. Of course, I wanted to go see him, but I had to ask Kurt for permission. He said no. He said I could go but not with Luke. I told him it would break my father's heart if I showed up without his grandson. I pleaded with him to understand how important it was for Luke to come with me.

"You can go, but Luke stays here," he repeated. Of course, I didn't need his permission to go on my own.

I said, "There's no way I can go without him."

To which Kurt coldly replied, "Well then your father will have to die alone."

I stayed put. I prayed that my father would not die until we could get there. I had to have faith that he would recover, and thankfully, he did.

The divorce dragged on. Court hearings were delayed, sometimes to deal with false allegations Kurt had made against me, sometimes for reasons I did not know. As time passed, our son was approaching school age. I was advised that if he started school in Germany, my chances of being able to leave with him would not be good. I needed a decision to be made—and fast.

But Spirit knew I wasn't ready. I hadn't yet learned the lessons I needed from this situation. Looking back, I can see them clearly:

1. I had to transcend the fear I felt and take back my power from Kurt.
2. I had to make peace with the present moment—be happy where I was.
3. I had to learn to trust in divine timing and let go of my own, which meant practicing patience.

Meditation helped me with all of the above. Connecting with that inner voice every day helped me to keep the faith that everything was unfolding as it was meant to. It connected me with the part of me that knows no fear. It also helped me to stay calm in the courtroom, even when Kurt and my lawyer were yelling at each other.

By January 2004, I got my miracle. The courts ruled in my favor, but my patience was tested further. Kurt appealed, which cost us another six months, but against all odds, we won a second time.

By this time, I had received the gift that patience brings—patience. I could've been angry and stressed with every day that passed, but thanks to my meditation practice, I was able to enjoy each day and trust that my son and I would be happy no matter what happened.

I knew that Spirit was taking care of us, and as long as I could get my fears and impatience out of the way (which meditation did for me every day), all would be well. I learned that faith and patience have a lot in common. Believing that something is coming for you means trusting that it will come, no matter how long it takes. And I understand now that getting impatient just makes it all take longer. It was when I let go and decided that it wouldn't be so bad if we had to stay in Germany after all that I won custody of my son. I had let go of my resistance, and the miracle came.

It was a precedent case, which ended up being printed in the law journals in Germany. Never before had a German court allowed a child of German descent to relocate with his non-German parent outside of the country.

When I got the news, I cranked up my stereo to the song "When You Believe" and sang my heart out. I knew deep in my soul that this was what I had sensed three years earlier, now coming to fruition. I understood why it couldn't have happened any sooner.

As long as I was afraid of Kurt, I was not free inside. By the end of those three years, I knew he could not harm me or our son. I knew from a deep place of knowing that all would be well in my life and that he had no more power over me. I felt compassion for him. I understood his fears that led him to desperate and destructive actions. I was even able to forgive him. That's when I knew I was free on the inside. And the Universe reflected that back to me by making me free on the outside as well.

Luke and I arrived in Winnipeg two weeks before school began. Packing up and shipping my things all happened like a whirlwind. Everything just worked out so smoothly that I knew I was being carried through the whole thing. I enrolled my son in a school that was a half hour drive from my father's house, hoping that I would eventually find a place to live nearby. By November, I found a cozy, little apartment just two blocks away. We called that home for the next five years.

Inspired Doing

A lot of people say to me, "This is all well and good with the meditation and belief, but a person still has to do something if they want to achieve a goal, don't they? God helps those who help themselves, right?"

Of course, that is the ego talking, and since we live in an ego-based society, 99 percent of others would likely say yes to that question. "Of course you have to do something! You can't just wait around and expect _____ to fall from the sky!"

Ye of little faith.

Here's the thing: sometimes what you need will just show up, without you having to do anything. Many times when I wondered how I was going to pay my rent, a check just showed up in the mail. When I was writing this book and my savings had run out, an inheritance came through (that had been in processing for about seven years)—right on time to keep me going for another few months!

And other times, you will need to do something. But it won't be an ego-based decision. It won't be out of fear that if you don't do it, your intention will not manifest. It will come from your intuition, and it may not even seem to have anything to do with your intention.

For example, you may feel like you really need to go to the mall one afternoon. Perhaps you're not a shopper. Perhaps you hate malls. Perhaps you look down on people whose hobby is shopping. But there is that little voice in your heart whispering, *Go to the mall.*

That doesn't seem like a very spiritual kind of inspiration. A lot of people might be inclined to ignore it. Not seeing the connection between going to the mall and finding the job of their dreams, they might decide to stay home and scroll through the job postings instead.

But if you'd gone to the mall, you might've run into an old friend. And that old friend might know someone who's just opened up their own business and is looking for someone with exactly your skills and experience. On top of that, the small company is in complete alignment with your values and vision for the world. Before long, you've landed your dream job, and it all happened because you listened to that little irrational whisper in your heart that told you to go to the mall!

Inspired doing will always lead you to where you need to be. Whether you want your dream job, perfect mate, ideal home, or a more slender figure, you can follow your ego's more direct-seeming approach, and you may even have success—for a little while. Or you can take the narrow gate and follow your inner voice down a possibly long and winding road, through situations that challenge you to grow and heal and learn who you really are. In my experience, this path leads to manifestations in your life that not only last but also are far better than the ones you hoped for or could've ever imagined!

SURRENDER AND LETTING GO

Can you step over the precipice, not knowing
what is below? Life starts this way.
—The Tao Is Tao, 17

The most important question a person can
ask is, is the Universe a friendly place?
—Albert Einstein

Surrender. This word scares people. It often gets interpreted as sacrifice, as if we're going to have to give up something we don't want to if we choose to surrender our ego. There is some truth to that, but surrendering your life to a higher power—whatever name you use for it—is something much more beautiful than that. The beauty of surrendering your ego is that you realize the things you were afraid to let go of were not the way to happiness anyway, so it ends up being a blessing to let them go, even if it's difficult at first. And in doing so, you clear the way for something much better.

So why is it so difficult for us to take this step?

I was leading a group one evening when the subject of receiving guidance from our inner voice came up. A woman said that she had asked a specific question in prayer, but no answer came; she wondered why. So I asked her whether or not she really wanted to hear the answer. Was she willing to accept whatever it was with all the consequences? She thought for a moment and with a little smile of having caught herself in the act, she said, "No."

I then posed the question to the others in the group: if you received guidance through meditation or prayer that involved you needing to leave your partner, quit your job, move to another country, or something similar, would you do it?

They all looked a little uncomfortable, and there were more little, knowing grins. They were honest enough with themselves to admit that they would not follow this guidance if it came to them. Understandable. These are drastic changes. But sometimes they're just the thing we need to change in order to find peace. The good news is we're not expected to just act on impulse with such guidance. All we need is to be open to the possibility, and the way will be shown to us, one small step at a time.

In the New Testament, Jesus tells the parable of the rich ruler who asks him what he has to do to inherit eternal life. Jesus tells him to sell everything he has and give the money to the poor and then to come and follow him. The man became very sad, so the story goes. Is Jesus asking him to do this because rich people can't find God? Is spirituality incompatible with financial success? I don't think so. I believe that what Jesus was challenging the rich man to do was to detach from his belongings, to let go of the belief that his happiness depended on having them. It is our *attachment* to the things and people in our lives that hinders our spiritual growth, not the things and people themselves.

Attachment breeds fear. If I am attached to something or someone in my life, it's because I believe it makes me happy. If I think I'm happy because of the job, partner, savings account, boat, house, family, or friends I have, then it is possible for my happiness to be taken away from me. Anything in the external world can fall out of our lives, no matter how much we think we are in control. We see it all the time. A marriage that seemed so stable ends. A rich man loses everything in the stock market crash or is unexpectedly laid off from his job. Fires burn homes to the ground. We see these things happen around us, and we live in fear of experiencing a similar twist of fate.

Fear is a manifestation of the ego. It's the part of us that wants things to stay the same. The ego is the part of us that clings to the status quo and screams, "Danger!" when change is in the air. Since change is inevitable, the ego is preventing us from being at peace by constantly fighting the inevitable. It convinces us that we can find ways of securing the things we don't want to lose, with various types of insurance and contracts. But ultimately, all of that just keeps us prisoners to our fears.

From one second to another, we are not the same people. We have different thoughts, feelings, even cells in our bodies, than we did a second ago. The sun is not in the same position, the weather has shifted, our kids have aged, and somewhere someone has passed on from this life as a new child is born. Change is the only thing we can count on. Yet we stubbornly fight it by clinging to things as they are. It even goes so far as people mourning the end of a television series. Is that really what you want to have determine your happiness? Everything in the Universe is always changing, and we cannot control these changes, no matter how hard we try.

We humans tend to feel that we have worked hard for what we have, and we are not going to walk away from it on a whim. The general consensus is not that we have what we have through the grace of a divine being but that we made it possible through our own plans, choices, and hard work. We don't like the idea of someone else being in control of our lives and often criticize people who believe in this as being fatalistic and lacking in drive or ambition. But this is inaccurate. We all receive guidance, but we still have the free will to choose to follow it or not. We are in control of that.

Living in a state of surrender does not mean that we sit around doing nothing all day, just hoping that somehow we'll be fed, clothed, and have our rent paid. It simply means that we include Spirit in our decision-making before we take action. For example, before deciding to apply for a new job, you might meditate and ask your higher self if you should. Sometimes guidance just feels like an idea we have, and surrender just means that we check in with our inner wisdom for confirmation before acting on it.

If you question the effectiveness of this approach, just remember that Mahatma Gandhi operated this way. He meditated—sometimes for days—before making his next move, and he managed to liberate an entire country without shedding one drop of blood. Ego-based decisions could not have achieved this, because they are too fraught with fear and doubt. When we check in with Spirit, we act on faith and a deep sense of knowing that can only come from within.

For most people in the Western Hemisphere, taking action based on Spirit guidance is for crazy people. I wonder if that's just a disguise for fear. Maybe we need to rationalize why we are not willing to let go of ego and let our lives be more Spirit led because we are afraid of giving up our feeling of control. Maybe we need to criticize those who are living this way because we secretly judge ourselves for not being able to.

And again, that's understandable because letting go of feeling in control is scary. Surrender sounds like I'm handing over the reins completely, but it's more accurate to say that I'm aligning my will with the will of the divine. I'm tuning in to what life wants for me and from me, and I'm directing my energy there. It sometimes means letting go of my own plans, but the result always brings me more joy and peace than my plans ever could have.

It would be impossible to surrender if our answer to Einstein's question at the beginning of this chapter were no. If you don't believe that the Universe is friendly, that your higher self wants you to be happy, that the divine loves you completely and unconditionally, then how can you let go and trust? If you start with letting go of control in little things, your trust will build. Eventually, you'll see that following that quiet voice in your heart can only lead you to happiness and peace. Sometimes it is not a straight path, but if you keep going, it is a sure thing.

I believe that divine will actually is my will, but I've forgotten it through all the conditioning, expectations, and distractions of the world around me. So surrendering doesn't mean that I give up what I want and choose what God wants, although many would phrase it that way. It means that I get in sync with my highest self to the point that I realize what the divine wants for me and from me is what I want as well. If I can let go of needing to please others and focus on pleasing God, I feel no conflict.

Most of us are so out of touch with our true selves that we can't believe our will and God's will could be the same. Most of us have no idea what God's will could be, and we are afraid to find out. We are afraid that following our highest self is going to mean sacrificing our own plans and comforts, so we don't even allow ourselves to think about what God's will for our lives might be.

Letting go of control is not an easy thing to do. We are taught to have a plan and to follow through with it. We are taught that if something goes wrong and we haven't created a safety net for ourselves, it's our fault. Those collective values of our society are in opposition to the soul-based approach, in which faith in a loving, generous provider is the only safety net needed. And contrary to the common belief that a good person finishes what they started, Spirit will sometimes ask us to walk away from a project we consider to be unfinished, because from a spiritual perspective, it has served its purpose.

We have to be constantly nurturing our faith if we choose to live in surrender. Ego is always waiting at the door, hoping for a moment of lower awareness where it can jump back in the driver's seat and tell you how crazy you were to think this approach to life could work. A lot of people try to follow an impulse or inspiration they feel is from Spirit, but they forget to continue a faith-building practice once they take the first leap.

When things don't work out, they conclude, falsely, that there is no higher power supporting them. What they don't understand is that they were the ones who allowed ego back in the driver's seat. Only a regular spiritual practice, like meditation, can ensure that this doesn't happen to you. Fears will always creep in, but the power of love will chase them away, if you choose it. If you want to live in surrender, it's an all or nothing deal. If you keep one foot in your secure, ego-driven life as you explore a Spirit-inspired path, it can't work. As long as fear is present, the power of faith is obstructed.

So why choose this kind of life? A lot of people would say they are very happy leading their ego-based lives. There's nothing wrong with having a plan that helps you achieve a comfortable lifestyle and wanting to enjoy the fruits of your labor. There's nothing wrong with wanting to stay with the partner you've been with for twenty years, because it feels comfortable and safe. There's nothing wrong with continuing in your current job even though it's not your passion, because it pays your bills. You can certainly live this way, and many people do.

But they're missing out.

Had the rich man in Jesus's parable been able to free himself from all his possessions and the lifestyle he was used to, he would have freed himself from fear. Fear is the only thing that ever blocks us from love. It's about facing our fears, not giving away our stuff or severing ties to our loved ones. It's about choosing love over fear so that you can find peace.

Jesus even promises, "… Verily I say unto you, There is no man that hath left house, or parents, or brethren, or wife, or children, for the kingdom of God's sake, Who shall not receive manifold more in this present time, and in the world to come life everlasting." (Luke 18:29–30). He's not saying, "Give it all away, and you'll be rich in the afterlife." He's saying, "Let go of the fear of losing what you have, and you will find peace here and now." The Buddha taught the same thing. All the spiritual masters got this. To let go of all that you are attached to, whether possessions, people, or plans, is to find a peace that surpasses understanding.

My Story

We had a lot of money in the bank by the time I left. I had sold my language school in Germany and invested the money I made. Kurt was earning very well since our move to France in his new position. Since he didn't like to spend much, it was accumulating. I recall wondering what the point was of having so much money in the bank as long as I felt I had to watch my spending so carefully. What freedom was there in having so much money? As far as I could tell, there wasn't any. In fact, I didn't feel free at all. Sure, we had financial security. Bills would get paid without any worry or struggle. In theory, I could buy whatever I wanted without having to worry about the price. But in practice, Kurt kept such strict tabs on my spending that even a cup of coffee had to be explained. "Where were you? With whom? Why couldn't you just wait till you got home to make one?"

Our baby was only nine months old when I realized I couldn't live this way anymore. Kurt threatened that he wouldn't pay a cent if I left, and I knew he meant it. Sadly, I knew that his attachment to his money was stronger than any feelings he had for me. That was why I had to go. Some part of me knew that there was more to life than feeling financially secure. Something inside me was longing for a life that I couldn't yet define, but I knew it was possible. And I knew I would not find it unless I took a leap of faith and left the life I'd settled for.

So that's what I did. Without an idea how I was going to support myself and my child, on a wing and a prayer, I walked away. I recall walking into a bargain store, holding my baby in my arms, and looking at their cheap, plastic kitchen utensils. I would need to start from scratch. It felt a little depressing to be back at this place after enjoying financial comfort for a few years. But my meditation practice helped me to hold on to the belief that better times would come.

The only true security comes from within, as any spiritual master will tell you. I found it time and again in my meditations, and that kept me going in those first weeks.

I had no plan, but I had a dream. I dreamt of freedom for my son and me. I dreamt that financial security was possible without having to forfeit personal freedom. I chose to believe that God wanted me to be happy, so no matter how scared I got at times, as long as I followed that little voice within, I would find that happiness. I didn't know how to get there, but I knew the first step I had to take was to leave.

At times like this, the phrase "let go and let God" is very powerful and real. I lived into each day, hoping, trusting, praying that all would be well. I often woke up afraid or with doubts, but after sitting in Presence for a few minutes, a deep knowing that all would be well came over me. There were ups and downs along the path, but overall life just kept getting better.

Then one day, sitting on the sofa in my new home, meditating after a phone call with my family back in Canada, my inner voice got through with a message I'd been too afraid to hear for a long time.

"I want to go home!" it said.

Home meant Canada. It meant I would have to face Kurt's wrath in a battle for permission to move away with our son. I had absolutely no desire to enter into that battle and could've contented myself with living in Germany for the rest of my life, had the voice of truth not spoken to me so clearly that day. The deep knowing was accompanied by sobs of relief at finally hearing what my heart longed for. God's will for me was not only that which would bring me great happiness and set me free. It also required that I speak up and ask for what I want in a way I'd never done before—that I put my needs before Kurt's. We often think of God's will as something that will ask us to sacrifice our own needs, not put them before others'!

I was terrified. But I obeyed my inner prompting, and the next few years brought about such growth and strength in me that I now refer to that period as my faith journey. All the world can be against you, but when you are carrying out God's will, you will succeed. The key is to keep the faith and take one step at a time. Leave the big picture to the universe and practice connecting to Source on a daily basis, so that your ego doesn't take over. Meditation was my main way of doing this, but singing in a choir and walks in nature also helped a lot.

The deep peace I felt once my sweet son and I were safely living in Canada can't be put into words. It was beyond anything I'd ever have dared ask for myself, but with God in the driver's seat, it's where I ended up. From that moment on, I vowed never to live by my ego again. God would stay in the driver's seat of my life because I now knew without a doubt that that was the way to find deeper peace and joy than I could ever achieve on my own. Without God, I am limited to what my ego tells me is possible, but with God I can achieve, create or overcome anything. Knowing this, I now live my life in a constant state of gratitude.

GRATITUDE

Acknowledging the good that you already have in
your life is the foundation for all abundance.
—Eckhart Tolle

Having an "attitude of gratitude" is quite a common phrase these days. Many people have tuned into the idea of keeping a gratitude journal or reminding themselves of things to be thankful for on a daily basis. This not only lifts our energies and makes us feel happier, it also attracts more into our lives to be thankful for. This is not to be confused with the pious attitude of being thankful in a "settling for what you have" kind of way. The attitude of gratitude I'm talking about means focusing on all the good in your life while simultaneously remaining open and receptive to more!

When we feel grateful for what we already have, we send out the energy of being fulfilled, of having. If we focus on what we want or do not yet have, we are sending out the energy of lacking. Of course, like attracts like, so the energy of having attracts more—not only things but also fulfilling experiences and relationships. It's the feeling of being satisfied that is repeated in this process, so anything that evokes this feeling in us can be manifested by the Universe, as long as we stay in gratitude.

When we focus our attention on the thing that seems out of reach, be it a new house, $10,000, or the love of our life, we stay in the feeling that happiness is just beyond our reach. Many people spend their whole lives waiting to be happy this way.

When I get a bigger house, I'll be happy.

If my husband was more like yours, I'd be happy.

When I lose weight, I'll be happy.

We don't realize that with this kind of thinking, we are constantly pushing happiness away. Instead of looking at what you don't have, you can feel happy now if you focus on what you do have. Gratitude for what you have now will attract more of the same, and life will become simply magical!

Sometimes it is advised to pretend that you already have the thing you want, and it will manifest. This is not about trying to trick the Universe, as some critics have said. It is about creating inside yourself the feeling of fulfillment that you would have if you already had the thing you desired. Our inner life creates our outer life, so if you can truly feel now the way you would if you had all those things you think you need, they will come! In fact, the beauty of this approach is that even if they do not manifest (because the Universe has something better in mind), you will be happy anyway. What more could you want? Often when you get to this point, you feel like it's not so important anymore to have the thing you wanted. And that is when it appears. When you release your ego attachment to getting something and choose to feel happy without it, it comes.

Sometimes, if we practice feeling grateful, we can make important discoveries about what might have been blocking us so far from receiving it. For example, if we really allow ourselves to be immersed in the feeling of gratitude for having $1,000,000, we might notice feelings of guilt cropping up. We might feel that we don't really deserve to have that much money when our parents had to struggle all their lives to make ends meet, for example. Or we might notice fear when we imagine losing our excess weight, because on some level we feel like it's protecting us. By simulating gratitude and discovering the blocks, we can get to work clearing them away, which opens us up to receiving. So the practice of feeling grateful even before we have what we want is a very powerful way of allowing it to manifest in our lives.

Even in situations that seem like bad luck or tragedy, it is possible to find something to be grateful for. It takes practice, but it is important that we do it so we don't spiral into the negativity of self-pity and suffering. Some will see this as a superficial behavior that avoids looking at the realities of life. New Age practitioners have sometimes fueled this fire by misunderstanding this concept.

Meditation is always about looking honestly at what we are feeling. The first feeling in an unfortunate situation is going to be pain, sadness, grief, or something similar. We don't want to wash over this with talk of gratitude. We need first to honor these feelings. Then, when we feel ready, we can start to look for something to feel gratitude about. If there truly is nothing in the situation that you can feel grateful for, find something outside the situation—simply to bring your energy back up!

The truth is, however, if you believe that everything happens for a reason and is part of the plan for your spiritual growth, you will be able to feel grateful even for something that those around you would consider negative.

I read a story of Chinese origin once about a wise farmer and his foolish neighbor. The wise farmer and his wife had a child, and the foolish neighbor rushed over to congratulate them. How wonderful that they had this baby boy! The farmer's reply was "Who can say what is good or bad?"

Years passed, and on the boy's sixteenth birthday, he received a beautiful horse. The foolish neighbor once again rushed over to admire the horse and tell the farmer how fortunate he was to have it. And the farmer replied, "Who can say what's good or bad?"

A few months passed when one day the boy was thrown from the horse and broke his leg. The foolish neighbor lamented this. "How terrible! You must be so upset! What an awful thing has happened to you!"

And the farmer calmly said, "Who can say what is good or bad?"

A week later, the army marched through the town, in search of young, strong men to go to war. Of course, with his broken leg, the farmer's son was no use to them, so he was allowed to stay at home.

Once again the foolish neighbor appeared to express his relief. "How fortunate you are that your son does not have to go to war!"

And once again, the wise farmer replied, "Who can say what's good or bad?"

The foolish neighbor allowed outer circumstances to determine how he felt, so he lived life on an emotional roller coaster. The wise farmer was centered within himself. He had a trust that everything was happening as it should, and he was able to transcend the need to judge things as good or bad. No matter what happened, he maintained his inner peace.

We can apply the same principle to staying in gratitude. No matter what is going on in your life, you can be grateful that the sun is shining. You can be grateful that your eyes work well enough for you to read the words on this page. You can be grateful for the bed you sleep in and for each breath you take, which nourishes your body with oxygen. As long as you can get into the vibrational feeling of gratitude, you will feel good, and good things will come your way.

Our egos want to point out to us everything that is going wrong in our days and make us focus on that. Regular meditation will help to quiet the ego and raise your vibration so that you more easily focus on the good that is already in your life.

The more often we connect with the invisible energies that are guiding and loving us, the more we will understand that we are truly never alone and that trusting this guidance will always lead us to greater happiness. When we reach this stage, things we once thought of as miracles become natural day-to-day events. The things we need, whether objects, insights, or people, cross our path just when we need them. We ask, and we receive. At this point, it is almost impossible *not* to live in a state of constant gratitude! And the best part is this authentic gratitude opens the door for even more blessings to flow in!

My Story

For years after the end of my marriage, I longed to find a partner who would truly love me. Understanding the principles above, I focused not on the lack of having a partner but on all the love that was already present in my life. Every day, I thanked the Universe for my beautiful son, for my friends and family. I felt happy to have the freedom to do what I chose when I wanted to. I tried to find the pros of being single rather than focus on the cons. I was happy with being single most of the time. Of course, the odd moment would hit where I felt it would be nicer to have someone at my side, but I didn't let myself wallow there for long. Life is in the present moment, and in the present moment, I had so much to be grateful for!

I didn't spend a lot of time making lists or vision boards of what my perfect partner would be. Instead, I focused on allowing myself to feel as beautiful, desirable, and loved as I would if I was already in the relationship of my dreams. Given my history with men, this was no easy task! Through meditation, I was able to connect with my Source and feel the greater love of which I am a part. From there, I was able to know that I am loved and to move into loving myself. It didn't happen overnight, but I began to feel truly grateful for being me—for being this loving, caring, beautiful woman God had made me into.

I was also grateful for the meaningful work that my inner growth had led me to. Not only did I get to spend my days helping others to find their paths and love themselves, but I was actually making enough money to support my son and myself doing it! Quite a few years had gone by, but I was far from frustrated at not having a partner. Every time I made another leap forward in my healing, I looked back and thought, *Thank God I didn't get into a relationship before clearing that away, or I'd have ended up right back in my old patterns of feeling unfulfilled in a relationship!*

More and more, I felt content with my independent life of being a self-employed, single mother. My son and I had a beautiful and peaceful life together. Only weeks before the man of my dreams walked into my life, I recall thinking, *Perhaps I am not meant to have another partner in this life. Maybe it's just going to be me, my son, and God.* And I was sincerely at peace with that.

At last, I was truly happy. The longing for a partner disappeared, and I felt fully committed to my life just the way it was. And of course, that's when Jon walked through the door.

I had set the stage, internally, for receiving a partner who would make me feel truly loved, and then I released the need to have him manifest. I was open to receiving but not attached to the outcome. I am grateful to the Universe for bringing Jon into my life but even more grateful that he did not come until I was ready. Only by doing the inner work to prepare myself have I been able to know that as happy as I am with him, I would be happy without him as well. This has allowed me a freedom in our relationship that I have never known before, and it feels wonderful.

Visualization

I've written about focusing on the end goal and letting go of trying to figure out how to get there, because this is where most people fall out of the flow. As soon as you try to take control of the process, you remove yourself from the path of least resistance. However, I am also aware that many teachers advise people to visualize steps toward the end goal, such as your perfect house, dream car, or ideal partner. So what are you supposed to do? Visualize having it or let it go?

As long as you to keep in mind that they are not the end goal (i.e., in and of themselves, they cannot bring you the deep, lasting peace and happiness that you desire), it is not wrong to visualize these things, but it might slow down your process of achieving them in the long run.

If your desire is to feel peace, and you visualize something that you mistakenly think will get you there (like a beautiful house on the coast), you may succeed in manifesting it, and you may even feel peace for a little while. However, if Spirit knows that your path to peace needs to involve living in a small apartment in downtown Toronto and learning to feel content there, then the house you manifested cannot last. Some twist of fate would remove it from your life, at which point many people might falsely conclude that the law of attraction doesn't work. The truth is Spirit sees the big picture that we usually cannot, and the house was not part of it, at least not at that point in time.

The other possibility is that you continue to try to manifest your idea (such as winning the lottery), but it simply doesn't work. You are convinced that all your problems would disappear if you could somehow manifest $100,000 into your life, so you make vision boards, do visualizations, and say affirmations all day long. When you don't win, you feel frustrated, exhausted, and start losing hope in the whole idea of cocreating your life. Maybe it's not working because you have a block within you, and working through this book will help remove it. Or maybe it's simply not for your highest good, and Spirit loves you so much that it is preventing you from going down this wide path that you think will lead you to happiness because it knows that what you will actually find is disillusionment, disappointment, and pain (as is the experience of many lottery winners).

So while it is not dangerous or wrong to focus on the steps toward your end goal rather than on the goal itself in your visualizations, you would save yourself a lot of energy and likely even some time by keeping your eye on the end goal of peace and letting the Universe lead you there.

In my classes, I encourage people to say, "This or something better is coming to me now," at the end of a visualization, so as to leave space for Spirit to intervene. I realize that an apartment in downtown Toronto may not seem like something better than beachfront property, but remember, if we knew better than Spirit how to achieve inner peace, we'd all probably have it already.

FORGIVENESS

*Forgiveness is unlocking the door to set someone
free and realizing you were the prisoner!*
—Max Lucado

*The weak can never forgive. Forgiveness
is an attribute of the strong.*
—Mahatma Gandhi

Why is forgiveness important in the law of attraction? We all have people who've hurt or disappointed us. We have people in our lives who we are angry with or resentful toward. In most cases, these feelings are absolutely justified and understandable. Tragically, many of us experience abuse, violence, and betrayal that hurt us deeply. The thought of forgiving people who've wounded us this way seems impossible, and yet if we don't, we remain stuck in that place forever.

Let me make absolutely clear that deciding to forgive someone is not in any way saying that what they did to you was OK. It was not OK, not even a little bit. But if you've been carrying anger, resentment, or pain around with you for years, you are not hurting the person who hurt you. You are only hurting yourself.

When you hold on to these feelings, you build a wall around your heart. The memories of your pain and sadness cause you to believe that you need to protect yourself at all costs from ever being treated that way again. Of course, on one level it is true that we need to protect ourselves, but building a wall around our hearts is the wrong way. It's motivated by fear, and all it leads to is a fear-filled existence.

If we close off our hearts, painful experiences will not have the same effect on us as they did when we were open and vulnerable, but neither will joyful ones. Do you feel that the level of joy and happiness you once knew as a child is gone and unattainable now? Has life gone from magical to mundane? Or perhaps you've never experienced the joyful innocence of childhood? Maybe your pain began at such an early age that you can't even recall the kind of happiness I'm speaking about. It doesn't matter. You can find it nonetheless, because it's still in you. It's in all of us.

A Course in Miracles (ACIM) says that there is a part of us, a divine spark within us, that remains untouched no matter what hardships or traumas we experience. Reading this gave me great hope at a very low point on my journey several years ago. It gave me the strength to persevere with my inner work even when I felt hopeless, when I felt like I was too broken to ever be put together again. I hung on to this idea that there was a part of me deep inside that was still whole, and eventually, I found it.

As we gradually reawaken that part of ourselves, we expand the part of us that feels whole and unafraid, which makes it easier to slowly let down the armor and open our hearts. Only by opening our hearts again can we heal from painful pasts and free ourselves to move forward in our journeys. If we do, we can discover or rediscover that joyful state that is our true nature and our birthright.

As discussed in chapter 5, we have to honor our pain first if we want to release it. My experience has been that if we don't heal our pain first, forgiveness cannot be real or lasting. So we need to do that work first. I have also realized that both the healing of the pain and the forgiveness of the other person seem to happen in layers, so don't expect to be done after the first time. It's OK to heal a little and forgive a little; heal a little more and forgive a little more …

Many people try to rush into forgiveness without honoring their pain first (including anger and tears), especially those who are attempting to lead a spiritual or religious life. This is called a spiritual bypass, as it leads us to a false sense of peace, which is really a form of denial. We want so badly to be done with the whole mess that we tell ourselves, "I've forgiven him/her! I'm moving on!" This is superficial at best unless we've sat with our pain and given space for our anger first. We need to allow ourselves the time it takes to properly heal, which will open our hearts and enable us to *truly feel* forgiveness for those who've hurt us. This can't be rushed.

Some say that forgiveness is grace. We can't make it happen. We can work on what's preventing us from wanting it, but when true forgiveness finally occurs, it's often like a wave washing over us at the most unexpected times. I love that.

Once we get closer to being willing to forgive, many of us will notice fear. I've had clients ask me, "Why don't I want to forgive this person? What's wrong with me? I know I should, but I can't!"

First, we need to take the pressure off and stop *shoulding* ourselves. Then we need to gently and patiently examine our hearts and minds to see what's blocking us. When we do, we will most certainly discover fear. After all, the reason we need to forgive in the first place is because we feel this person (or group of people) hurt us. Holding on to unforgiveness gives us the illusion that we are protected, so they can't hurt us again.

The catch is that as long as we believe this, we are not only living in a constant state of underlying fear, but we are also allowing our personal power to be in the hands of others. Can you imagine? The very person you trust the least is the one you're handing the reins of your life to, every day that you refuse to forgive them.

"If I don't forgive you, you can't hurt me again!" is what we think is happening. The reality is, "If I don't forgive you, I keep the pain, fear, and anger alive inside me, and they block me every minute of the day and night from allowing all the love and abundance into my life that the Universe has for me."

Exercise

Pain begets pain. The people who've hurt us were unconsciously projecting their own pain onto us, and we accepted it at the time. Many of us continue to hold onto our parents' pain, for example, because we would feel guilty if we gave it back to them. The truth is you're not helping anyone by carrying their pain. You're preventing them and yourself from healing and growing into the beings you are meant to be. Giving someone back their pain is an exercise you can do on your own; you need never confront them. It is a very powerful way of lightening the load you've been carrying.

Sit in front of a mirror. Have a box of tissues and a large cushion handy. Look into your own eyes and say to the person you need to forgive, "(Name), you hurt me deeply and caused me a lot of pain in the past. However, I am not willing to stay stuck in the past. That is why I am handing you back your pain today. I am no longer willing to carry it.

"As I return your pain to you, I pray that you will find the strength and courage to heal. But healing is a choice, and regardless of what you choose to do, my choice is to let go of this pain.

"I forgive you for what you did to me and I release you. I now sever the bond of pain that connected us and free myself. You are free, and I am free."

Stay there in front of the mirror and take a few more conscious breaths. If tears come, let them flow. These are healing tears. If anger arises, yell, punch, or squeeze a cushion or whatever else you might feel like doing instinctively (as long as it does not cause damage to anyone). You might also want to use the cushion to scream into.

Whatever feelings are arising, let them be there. They've been pushed down long enough. It's time to acknowledge and release them so that you can move forward with your life.

My Story

When I left Kurt, he was very angry. Having taken me away from the support of my friends and with our infant son, I suppose he thought he'd gotten me to the point that I would not be able to leave him. It was a scary thing to do with a nine-month-old child in my arms, but the prospect of what would happen to me if I stayed in an abusive and controlling relationship frightened me more.

I had tried everything to improve our relationship, but I had to admit to myself that it was never going to improve, because he was fine with the way things were. His needs were being fulfilled, and mine were not important. My heart and spirit felt broken from the years of physical and emotional neglect, psychological abuse, and constant criticism. I was a shadow of my former self, depressed and completely lacking in self-confidence.

With the help of meditation and rebirthing therapy, I found the strength to walk away, trusting in God to take care of my son and me. I didn't want my son growing up with a depressed mother. I didn't want him to have to bear that burden. I couldn't be happy in a relationship where I was constantly being broken down, so I had to leave.

As I said, he didn't see it coming. The first year or so after I left, he was surprisingly pleasant and cooperative. The return of Prince Charming. We talked about the possibility of getting back together, so he was on his best behavior. Then one day we had an argument in which I said angrily, "And that's why I will *never* get back together with you!"

That was the moment the mask came off.

It seemed to me that from that point on, his main goal in life was to make me as miserable as possible. I feared losing my son, feared for our physical safety and our financial future. Kurt was devious in trying to make me look mentally unstable (i.e., unfit to be a mother) in front of the social workers, and he seemed to have no problem using our son to manipulate me. He would do things that hurt or upset our child and then blame me for them. I felt like I had to be constantly on my guard, as he was setting traps for me, and if I slipped up, I could lose my son.

One day he went so far as to physically assault me. He threw me onto the ground in front of his apartment and then threw himself on top of me with all his weight. He'd hit me before, but this was a whole new level. To make matters worse, our son was in the car right beside us, crying. I managed to get out from under him and ran toward the car door, but he ran around the other way and blocked me from getting in, with a maniacal grin on his face.

The only thing I could think to do was to yell for help, and as soon as I did, he ran off and hid in his apartment. Later, in court, he would present two affidavits that claimed I had been the attacker and he was the victim. One was from his new girlfriend's friend, and the other was from a neighbor, who later told me that she had not seen all that happened and that he pressured her into signing it, which she now regretted.

I had every reason to hate this man, or at least to be very angry with him. But I was on my spiritual journey by then, and I knew that staying angry with him kept me linked to him. More than anything, I just wanted freedom for myself and my son from this toxic person.

I filed for divorce shortly after he became hostile (which fueled the fire), but it had been almost two years already, and things were moving slowly. I was asking for permission to move to Canada with our son so that I could work (in Germany, I could only work on temporary work permits, and he was threatening to sabotage the renewal process) and be financially independent from this controlling man.

I asked myself why it was taking so long, and through meditation, it became clear to me that I had left him physically a few years earlier, but emotionally, he still had the same control over me as before. He was able to scare me with his threats and anger as well as make me feel guilty if things didn't go his way. I saw that if I wanted to be truly free of him, I had to be free of all these emotions that connected me to him.

I got to work in my meditations, releasing guilt and fear. (Disclosure: I suppressed the anger for the time being, as I was attempting to remain positive about his father toward my son, but it came up again years later, and I have since managed to acknowledge and let that go as well.) In looking closer at my fear, I was able to see that he, too, was afraid. In sitting with my pain, I saw that he, too, was hurting. Violence and anger were the only way he knew how to express it. I could feel my heart soften toward him.

The next time he came to my door and made his usual comment about me trying to come between him and his son, rather than react from my fear, I looked him in the eyes with an open heart and asked, "How can I help you to not be so afraid of that? I want you to have a good relationship with our son."

It was amazing to see the change in his demeanor. Immediately, it was like he dropped his armor, and we were able to speak to each other in a civil manner for the first time in a long time. We didn't solve all our problems right then and there, but we made an important step.

More importantly for myself, I learned at that moment just how powerful love is. As long as I stayed afraid of him, he had power over me. As long as I allowed his actions to upset me, I could not meet him from my highest self.

When I was able to see him with love and compassion, I could see that in his own way, clumsy and destructive though it was, he was trying to get love and approval himself. He needed people to think highly of him, and my leaving had threatened that image, so he had to paint me as the crazy one, the bad guy. He had made our divorce into a war in which only one of us could win. As long as I fought back, the war continued.

Once I saw more clearly what was happening, I stopped fighting. I didn't give in, and I certainly didn't decide that what he did to me was OK. His behavior was deplorable, and I did not deserve to be on the receiving end of any of it. But I no longer wanted to stay linked to him this way. I just wanted to be free. Through meditation, I transcended the situation from the level of ego reactions and approached it with soul awareness. Seeing his higher self with my higher self was what made it possible to forgive him. In the end, we are all the same and want the same things.

It was a profound lesson for me. What I understood was that love was the greatest protection of all, because it disarms your perceived enemy. Love reminds us that we are all one and that there is nothing to fear.

I stopped fighting and continued in my meditations to keep an open heart. Less than two weeks later, the court decision finally came through. Inner freedom had to be achieved before outer freedom could. Internal creates external. It's true in every case. When I felt free inside, I was granted primary care of our son and, with it, the right to decide on his place of residence. The report literally said that it "trusted in the good judgment of the mother" to make that decision. How can that be the work of anyone else but Spirit?

When I opened my heart to my ex-husband in forgiveness, I let down the walls that were blocking me from receiving what the Universe wanted for me. It is clear today that I was meant to move back to Canada and that everything for my son and me has unfolded just as it was meant to. Had I been unwilling to forgive his father, I would likely still be living in Germany, still fighting, still linked to him through toxic emotions. I know many people whose divorce anger goes on and on for years. They are making it difficult for good things to come to them and are keeping themselves in an unnecessary state of stress and suffering.

Forgiveness is the way out of that. The only way.

Stop Complaining!

Do you ever find yourself doing something and thinking, "Why should I have to do this? I did this the last time. I have to do everything around here!"

I'm sure we have all experienced this at some point, and if we are aware enough of our thoughts, we have noticed it. It's a tendency we all have, and we have to make the conscious effort to rein it in so that we don't get sucked into it. Why?

Because complaining is negative energy, and like attracts like. Once again, it's not the person you are complaining about who is being damaged the most when you grumble about them; it's you!

I try to live by a simple motto: if there's a task to do and I don't feel like doing it, I don't. Our natural, healthy rhythm is to have periods of rest and activity throughout the day, according to yogic philosophy. Most societies today run on a nine-to-five schedule, which throws this balance completely off. We find ourselves feeling forced to do things when we don't feel inclined to do them—or worse, doing them with bitterness. How can that be healthy?

I have found that if I allow myself to have the break or the little rest that my natural rhythm is asking me for, it doesn't take long before I actually feel like getting those dishes done, making that phone call, or finishing up that report. We are not inherently lazy. We just feel that way sometimes because we're forcing ourselves to work without respecting our need to rest in between.

Of course, the voices in our heads are saying right now, "Well, sometimes things just have to get done! I can't afford the luxury of waiting till I'm in the mood!"

I admit, sometimes this is the case, though not as often as you may be convincing yourself. First, I would ask you to check in with yourself and find out how urgent it really is to get this thing done—and why. Is it really necessary to clean the kitchen floor again because your mother is coming for a visit if you just mopped it two days ago? Sometimes we create our own stress because we attach too much importance to what others think of us (see chapter on self-love once more if this is you).

If you answer the above question honestly and the answer is still yes, it has to be done now, then the next step is simple: choose to do it with a positive attitude. I said simple, not easy.

We have to train our minds to be more positive; it's not going to happen by itself. So you have to decide that if you're going to be the one cleaning out the car or doing all the grocery shopping by yourself again, you'll find a way to enjoy it. You'd be surprised at how easy it is to do that, once you've had some practice, and at how much better you feel.

JUDGMENT

Judge not, that ye be not judged.
—Matthew 7:1

The prevailing attitude in our society/religious teachings has been that judging others is a bad thing. We are warned not to do it because we'll be punished or judged ourselves if we do. This attitude seems like a warning or a threat rather than the good advice that it should be. And it hasn't worked too well, because as far as I can tell, not many people get through the day without passing judgment on those around them.

"He is so lazy. He didn't deserve to get that promotion."

"My brother is such a loser!"

"Her new haircut looks awful!"

"What an a--hole driver!"

"My boss is an idiot."

You might be thinking, those statements don't sound that bad. And besides, they're true!

To you they are, because that is your perception, but to me, they may not be. Each one of us creates our own stories and opinions about the world around us and believes it to be the truth (more on that in the next chapter).

If you are judging others, you are attracting negative energy to yourself. I don't think Jesus (in the quote above) was threatening us with punishment for judging others. I think he was trying to teach us that we attract to ourselves the very thing that we send out into the Universe. I think that he understood that in judging others, we are actually judging ourselves.

It's not a moral question. It's much simpler than that. Do you want to be happy? Then listen to me now. When we judge others, whether in our thoughts or with our words, we are emitting negative energy. When we emit negative energy, we attract negative energy. It's like a boomerang. This energy can express itself in many ways—physical pain, sadness, trouble in relationships. There are many ways it can show up, but the one thing that is certain is that it will show up, and it will not feel good.

So the bottom line is this: if you want to feel good, stop judging other people.

Why do we judge?

Some would say that judging is a normal and necessary thing to do. Obviously when there is a huge truck speeding toward us, we need to judge the situation as dangerous, so we can get out of the way. We need to judge between the value of vegetables as opposed to doughnuts to nourish our bodies. We can objectively say the speeding truck is dangerous and the vegetables are better for us.

But there's another kind of judgment that is not so objective. In fact, it's very personal. The kind of judgment that emits negative energy is the kind that stems from a need to feel better than others. It only happens if we don't feel good about ourselves, and that's a negative state of mind to be in. So it's not even so much about the act of judging as it is about the intention behind the act, which is self-rejection. If you need to judge others to feel better about yourself, how receptive can you be to all the good in the Universe?

Many of us suffer from a feeling that we are not good enough as we are. In a misguided attempt at feeling better about ourselves, we try to find fault in those around us. Our egos would have us believe that putting them down will somehow lift us up, but the opposite is true. We may temporarily feel better about ourselves with this approach, but that negative vibe is making its way back to us, and by the time it arrives, we will likely be oblivious to our own role in creating it.

Here's what I've noticed. If I am having an insecure body image day and I see someone who is in worse shape than me, I will use that to make me feel better. Perhaps I see someone who is younger and heavier than me. Then I can say, "Hey, for my age, I look great!"

Then I walk around the corner and come across a person who is at least ten years older than me and sporting a designer outfit that is at least three sizes too small for me to ever hope to squeeze into! Now what?

Well, if I've allowed myself to be in the mindset of feeling better than the first person, it will be impossible to avoid feeling worse than the second one. Why? Because I've given power to my ego, which can't help but compare. That's what ego does—what it was conditioned to do. The only way out is to transcend my ego state of mind.

This is no easy task, especially in the moment it's happening, but if I can achieve this, I will be able to feel good about myself no matter how I size up against others.

The way to feel better about ourselves is not to judge and compare in either direction. That can never work. As in the poem, "Desiderata," "If you compare yourself with others, you may become vain and bitter, for always there will be greater and lesser persons than yourself."

It is hard to work on accepting yourself when the ego is tempting you to compare and judge instead. It takes discipline to choose the path of transcending ego in our moments of insecurity.

However, unless we consciously work toward a more soul-based approach to life, we can't help having judgmental thoughts go through our heads all day long. Ego will always try to prove that you are better or worse than those you're judging. Yes, we judge the ones we feel inferior to as well.

"Skinny bitch! She probably starves herself to look like that!"

"He's so full of himself with his fancy new car!"

"Who does she think she is?"

The ego tells you that you're not good enough. Society's values might tell you that these people are somehow better than you. That's why you have to break them down. If they get the praise and attention, you won't. If they are loved, there will be none left for you. That's the lie of ego—the illusion that most of us have spent our entire lives living under.

Meditation is the way to transcend the ego and practice seeing who you really are, beneath all the insecurities that cause you to judge others. It shows us that we are all connected, so we can sincerely be happy for another person's success. Meditation helps us move from a competition mentality to a feeling of unity and cooperation, which leads to compassion, rather that criticism, of ourselves and others. And one day, we may even be able to see through the illusion of separateness and realize that we are all one, all connected. So when you judge someone else, you are always judging yourself.

Exercise

At this point, you might be thinking, *I'm not judgmental! I do my best to say only kind things.*

That's great, if it's true. But it's not the whole picture. Subconsciously, we all carry beliefs that can be very judgmental in their nature. If they are there, then you are consistently sending out negative energy without being aware of it, and that is affecting your life.

So let's have a look at what's hiding in your psyche, shall we? As spontaneously as possible, without censoring or trying to impress anyone, finish the following phrases:

1. People who beat their children are _____.
2. Obese people should/shouldn't _____.
3. I think vegans are _____.
4. People who don't recycle are _____.
5. I can't stand _____.
6. Politicians are _____.
7. I wish people weren't so _____.
8. It is wrong to _____.
9. People who are always late _____.
10. Rich people _____.

If you were honest with yourself, you'll have noticed at least half of your phrases were negative. The point of seeing this is not to feel criticized. It is to shed light on the ways we are unconsciously sending negative energy into the Universe. You want to be happy, right? Then you need to become aware of these chronic judgments as well as the acute ones we looked at earlier. Whether it's in a particular situation or a long-standing opinion, if it's judgmental, it is going to bring negative energy into your life.

Becoming more aware of our tendency to be judgmental of others may surprise those of you who considered yourselves to be very open and accepting. Resist the temptation to judge *yourself* for this and instead make it a regular practice to be more aware of what you're thinking. As you uncover your hidden judgments, practice compassion toward yourself. Remember, you weren't born with those thoughts in your head. They were programmed into you through the situations and people you grew up with.

Meditation is a powerful practice for shedding light on the nature of our thoughts and words, so that we can make them more positive. This is so powerful in cocreating our lives that I advise you to not only stop a negative judgment if you notice one but to take the next step and make it a positive one instead.

So instead of saying, "She should not be wearing a dress that short at her age!" we might say, "I admire her confidence to wear a dress that short at her age and not let society dictate what she should or should not wear."

And instead of "People who beat their children are monsters!" we might say, "People who beat their children need help. I want to have more compassion for whatever causes them to behave this way."

My Story

My first experience of Kurt being tight with his money came within the first week of our living together. I came out of the shower one morning to find him visibly agitated. We'd just come back from spending time at my father's house in Canada, and I guess he'd observed that we took longer in the shower than he was used to. Now, back in Germany, he was letting me know that he would not tolerate that kind of extravagance.

"I don't know how your father does it, but I'm not going to spend half my paycheck on hydro bills!"

I was truly surprised, as my shower had only been about ten minutes. The time it takes to wash, condition, and rinse out my long hair was surely more than he needed, but I didn't feel like I took longer than I needed. Still, I apologized and said I would try to be faster in the future. I wasn't earning any money yet, as I'd just moved back from three months in Canada, so I didn't feel that I had the right to argue.

In my years before being with Kurt, even though I didn't make a lot of money, I enjoyed going out with my friends for dinner often. I preferred to spend time sitting in a restaurant for hours talking, laughing, and enjoying good food together, rather than buying things, so what little money I made went mostly toward eating out, once my bills were paid.

Well, that was the second situation that showed me how very differently we viewed money. When I suggested we go out for dinner, Kurt said he didn't think going out to eat was worth the money you paid. He preferred to eat at home. A few months later, when I'd begun earning some money myself, I insisted that we join some of my friends for dinner one night. Kurt came along grudgingly and ordered only soup. I felt so embarrassed. All my friends were ordering full meals and drinks, as we always did. Kurt ate his bowl of soup and leaned back in his chair, not making any attempt to interact with the rest of us. I nervously tried to bring him into the conversation a few times, but he was uncooperative. I was so ashamed that I never asked him to join me and my friends for dinner again.

I was teaching English, and as my clientele grew, so did my income. A year or so later, I was at the point that I would go out with my friends on my own, spend my own money on dinner, and talk openly about how stingy he was. I would share stories like how he got mad at me for buying a block of cheese at the regular supermarket and not the discount mart we usually went to; how he didn't want to stop for a coffee on our weekend trip because he thought it was too expensive; how he'd get angry with me if I gave money to someone living on the streets and say, "If you have too much money, give it to me!"

It was a coping behavior of mine to share these stories. Laughing at his greed made living with it somewhat more bearable. But of course, I wasn't doing myself any favors. By complaining about him and judging his attitude toward money, I was attracting a lot of negative energy to myself without realizing it. It's no wonder our relationship got worse as time went by. I focused on all the things he wasn't and all the negative things he did. He, in turn, criticized me more and more. We were spiraling ourselves further and further down the hole into darkness and didn't see it.

A few months before I left him, I began seeing a therapist. We used a breathing technique called rebirthing to help me bring things out of my subconscious mind, out of the darkness and into the light. It was a very powerful technique and led me to becoming more accepting of myself. This resulted in more tolerance and understanding toward everyone around me. I felt like the foggy, confused state my mind had been in for as long as I could remember was finally clearing. I was seeing everything with more clarity and insight.

After I left him, I gradually began to understand why Kurt was the way he was with money. Both of his parents were children during World War II. They both had traumatic experiences, which included losing all their possessions and not knowing where their next meal would come from. Somehow, they made it through all that and managed to find each other and create a new life and family of their own.

But they never fully recovered. They lived very frugally and managed to save up enough money to give their children a good life. They invested and saved so that when their kids went off to study, they were able to support them. They almost never went out to eat and avoided luxuries of any kind.

Even in our time together, Kurt's mother would make zucchini every night for about a month in September, because that was what they had in the garden. By this time, they could have easily afforded to give some away and buy a different vegetable to have some variety, but that was not part of her thinking. Kurt never complained about his mother's frugality. He was very protective of her. He saw her as a fragile, anxious person who had gone without in order to provide for her kids. No wonder he couldn't enjoy his money!

Not only had they given each of their children thousands over the years, but even the money he was making now was only possible because they'd paid his way through university. It seemed to me that somehow Kurt's parents' feeling that no matter how much money they had, they were never really safe had been passed down to him. Even with hundreds of thousands of dollars in the bank, he still behaved as if he were poor. It wasn't greed as such, I realized. It was fear.

With this deeper understanding of where Kurt's attitude toward money had come from, I was able to stop judging him as greedy and began praying for him to be freed from these fears instead. I don't know whether it has made any difference in his life, but I know that I have felt more at peace ever since.

Blame

Most people see external things as the cause of their predicament. For example, we tend to blame everything from our jobs to our children when we feel stressed. When a relationship ends, we usually see the fault in the other person. A fight with a friend—she's the problem!

What we don't realize is that by blaming others, we are missing out on the opportunity for spiritual growth. Understanding the law of attraction is not about blaming yourself; it is about taking back your power. When you understand what your part was in cocreating a certain situation in your life, you can change it!

You don't have to complain about or try to change another person so that you can be happy. Just change the belief that attracted that situation, and it will cease to appear in your life. Yes, it's that simple!

PROJECTION

Everything that irritates us about others can
lead to an understanding of ourselves.
—Carl Jung

There is another very important aspect in the theme of judgment, and that is projection. If we want to understand ourselves better and get control of our judgmental thoughts, we need to have a closer look at what projection is all about.

To project means to see in someone else a quality or behavior that we don't want to see in ourselves. The human psyche possesses the ability to relegate aspects of the self that it doesn't like to the darkness, otherwise known as your shadow self. This is where we keep those parts of ourselves that we would vehemently deny being. Zen teacher Cheri Huber writes, "What we find difficult or unacceptable 'out there' is nothing more than a projection outward of what we have been taught to find unacceptable in ourselves."

So let's say Cathy was taught at a young age that she had to keep her home impeccably clean in order to be a good woman/wife. Now, as an adult, she finds it impossible to relax with a good book or watch TV when there are dirty dishes in the sink. Others complain that she should just relax and enjoy her tea after dinner, rather than jumping up to clean right away, but she can't. Deep in Cathy's psyche is the belief that she would be a bad person if she didn't keep everything clean. She is held prisoner by this belief and doesn't even know it. In Cathy's conditioned mind, she is simply doing things the right way; the good way.

Now if Cathy were to visit her friend Tracy, whose parents taught her that life is about having fun first and house work can always wait, she would have a hard time with that. Let's say Tracy had a big dinner party the night before, and as Cathy arrives, there are still dirty dishes all over the kitchen. Tracy can ignore it and enjoy her visit, but Cathy can't sit still in the mess and soon offers to help clean it up. This annoys Tracy, who would rather spend quality time with her friend now and clean up later.

Cathy's thought would be *Tracy is so lazy! I don't know how she can sit in the middle of that filth and visit as if it weren't there! I could never do that!* (Undertone: *I am better than Tracy.*)

Tracy's thought would be *Cathy is so uptight! Why can't she just loosen up and bit and enjoy the moment, like me?* (Undertone: *I am better than Cathy.*)

Which one of these women do you identify with more? Who's right and who's wrong here? Whatever your answer, all it shows is how you were conditioned. There is no right or wrong. There's only conditioning.

The truth is there's a deeply buried party of Cathy that would love to be more like Tracy. She may not be aware of it and likely could never admit it, but it's there, hiding. If anyone ever asked Cathy if she wanted to be like Tracy, she'd deny it vehemently. It's unimaginable for her to be that way. And it drives her absolutely crazy that Tracy can not only live the way she does but also seems to be happy doing so!

All the while, Tracy's got her own little secret envy going on. As uncool as it would seem, Tracy would actually like her home to look more like Cathy's at times. But her upbringing was more chaotic and less structured, and she simply does not possess the organizational skills to keep her home as impeccable as Cathy's. So she pretends she doesn't want it and judges Cathy for having it. If she doesn't see Cathy as uptight, she'd have to see herself as incapable, and that, to Tracy, is unacceptable.

This is just one example of an unconscious behavior that repeats itself in infinite variations between people with different conditioning every day. Cathy is seeing in Tracy her own hidden desire to just let things go and relax sometimes, and Tracy is seeing in Cathy her own hidden desire to be more organized and efficient at keeping her home clean. Both are projecting their inner judgments of these qualities onto each other. If it's not acceptable in me, it's not acceptable in her!

The solution to this is simple but not easy. If Cathy could allow herself to relax a little, and Tracy could give herself permission to be more organized, each without judging herself, the need to judge the other would just fade away. Or, in fact, neither of them needs to even change their behavior. Simply accepting that she would like to be a little more like her friend at times would free each of these women from the need to judge each other. But that's hard when you've banished that desire to your shadow.

That's why learning to love and accept ourselves first is so important. That's what is meant when people say you can't really love anyone else if you don't love yourself. You will always find things to judge about other people until you accept all of you.

More on Projection

And it can get even more interesting than that. Life has a way of making us look at what we don't want to see—making us honest. Yes, it will annoy you to be around people who display the qualities in you that you reject. But if there's no one around who actually possesses those traits, the power of projection will make you see them anyway. Even if the other person is not even slightly the way you are seeing them, you will be convinced that your perception is accurate.

If you refuse to see that you can be a bit of a know-it-all, you'll be surrounded by people who you perceive to be know-it-alls. If you are uncomfortable with your anger to the point that you pretend it's not there, you'll find yourself constantly dealing with angry people. In these cases, it is entirely possible that the people in question are not know-it-alls or angry at all! But until you accept these aspects of your own shadow self, you'll insist that they are.

I can hear some of you now, saying, "I'm surrounded by greedy people, but I'm very generous!"

"My coworkers drive me crazy because they're lazy. Does that mean I am lazy? Ridiculous!"

In reality, we are all both sides of the coin. We all have moments of generosity and moments of greed. We can all be both lazy and hardworking. It's our spiritual work to integrate the two opposites in order to find wholeness. Only when we try to reject those parts of ourselves are we forced to deal with them in others.

This may be hard to accept, but it's actually an opportunity for growth. If we fail to see this, we will spend our entire lives struggling and frustrated with other people. But if we accept the challenge to look within instead of pointing fingers, we can find the source of our projection and choose to accept that part of ourselves. Once integrated, these qualities or behaviors no longer need to manifest on the outside for us to see them, so our relationships become easier and more harmonious.

Through regular meditation, you will learn to see yourself more honestly. With practice, it will become easier to own your projections. At first, this may feel challenging, but as you see the resulting peace in your relationships, you will be more inclined to look within whenever you feel upset with someone else. You will gradually find that you can say, "I may be chaotic/stingy/angry/lazy/uptight some of the time, but I still love myself!" When you stop judging yourself, judgmental thoughts about others will disappear.

Exercise

This exercise is very simple.

Think of someone who really annoys you—not just someone you don't like but someone who drives you crazy. Maybe the very sound of their voice grates on you.

Now write down five to ten words to describe this person.

Circle the three that you think are strongest and most accurate.

Now take a deep breath and ask yourself if you can also be that way sometimes. Don't just take your knee jerk response to this question. Dig deep. Be open.

For example, if you wrote that your mother drives you crazy because she's always meddling in other people's business, ask yourself, "Do I sometimes stick my nose where it doesn't belong?"

If you wrote that your coworker drives you nuts because she's so disorganized and irresponsible, ask yourself, "Is there a part of me that would like to be less in control and a little more relaxed about things?" Or perhaps you are a little disorganized yourself, and you feel ashamed of that. Can you love that part of you instead?

This exercise takes some brutal honesty with ourselves, but if we can do it, not only will the relationships in our lives improve, but we will also become more balanced, less reactive individuals. As we learn to accept every aspect of ourselves, we will attract others into our lives who are also more accepting and easier to be with.

My Story

To continue with the story in the last chapter, as I began to learn about the law of attraction, I asked myself why I had attracted a man who was so tight with his money. I never thought of myself as stingy. In fact, I was the one who readily gave to those in need! I very much wanted to reject the idea that I might have attracted a stingy partner into my life because I myself was stingy. That was simply not true. That was not how I saw myself; nor was it how I wanted to see myself.

If I judged Kurt for his tightness with money and even ridiculed him with my friends, what would I have to think of myself if it turned out that I was that way too? Impossible! There was no way I could allow that and still be able to live with myself.

"That's not me!" said my ego. "That's him! I'm the one who wants to go out for dinner! He's the one who says it's too expensive! He's the problem—not me!"

Thanks to meditation, I was able to quiet the voice of my ego, and gradually the truth began seeping through. I realized that, while I did go out with my friends for dinner almost every night before meeting Kurt, I was usually the one at the table who spent the least. This was not because I was cheap, mind you, but because I simply did not have a lot of money.

I was working as an ESL teacher in a small private school. The pay was all right, but sometimes there were more hours available than others, so I could never be sure from month to month how much I would earn. This caused me to be very careful with my money, so while my friends were ordering one drink after another, I would make mine last all evening. While they ordered expensive meals with extra sides, I would stick to the lower-priced items on the menu.

Of course, this isn't where my belief in scarcity began. From my earliest days, I recall my parents arguing over money—or lack of it. My father sometimes spent recklessly, and my mother would be upset because she was struggling to stretch every dollar she spent on groceries.

We were a family of seven, and we lived off only one income—my father's salary as a junior high school teacher. Although there was always enough to eat, there was not a lot leftover for extras like going out to eat. Clothing was bought once a year at the beginning of the school year. I would get a new pair of jeans, shoes, and perhaps a sweater. If I wanted more than that from the age of about twelve on, I purchased it with the money I made from babysitting.

The designer clothes many of my high school friends enjoyed were a far-off dream for me.

Fortunately, with my two older sisters and my mother's wardrobes to help out, I managed to stretch my own. We borrowed back and forth, I got hand-me-downs, and I bought the odd new item from one of the cheaper department stores.

Needless to say, abundance was not part of my belief system.

Scarcity was the only experience I'd ever had with money, so although I didn't consider myself to be cheap, I gradually began to see that I had a lot of fear around the subject of money. I was even proud of my ability to make do, make a meal when the cupboards seemed bare, or make an old, worn-out bookshelf look attractive by throwing a nice shawl over it and decorating it with little trinkets or cards I had.

When I got a present like candles or any kind of bath products, I would hold on to them forever. I was afraid to use them, afraid of not having them anymore once they were gone. I recall getting a small bottle of scented massage oil from a friend once. Not wanting to use it up, I put it on a shelf and saved it (for when?). I opened it up once and used a tiny bit. Then I left it for quite a while again, thinking it too precious to use up all at once.

By the time I went to use my lovely scented oil again, it had gone rancid. The lovely smell was overpowered by the putrid smell of oil gone bad. I was so disappointed, and at the same time, I was grateful for the lesson.

I'd put off the enjoyment of this small luxury for so long that I lost it completely. From that day on, I vowed to let go of that scarcity mindset and to start enjoying the little pleasures in life whenever I could. Not only would I use a gift like that sooner these days, I also buy them more often for myself now!

So it was my own belief in lack that was lurking in my shadow self. I didn't want to see myself as greedy, cheap, or stingy. I thought of my frugal ways as a virtue. I think deep down I felt that my mother would approve of my approach to money. I was nothing like my extravagant father, whom she so often criticized for his spending habits. And I wanted to be nothing like him. I wanted my mother's approval. Just like Kurt wanted his mother's approval.

We weren't so different after all. I'd attracted a man who was afraid to enjoy his money, so that I could finally see myself. He seemed to be more extreme than I, and maybe he was. I think the Universe brings us magnified versions of ourselves so that we will finally see the truth. The point, however, was not who was more afraid. It was that I would never attract a generous partner or abundance in any form until I acknowledged my own fear of not having enough. As

I got to work on that, I gradually saw the changes in my life. A belief in abundance has created a comfortable life, attracted a generous partner, and allowed me to enjoy all the little pleasures that come my way.

But most importantly, accepting the uncomfortable truth about my own fears around money has helped me to stop judging not only Kurt but anyone else I meet who seems hesitant to part with theirs. It has made me more compassionate, as I understand that behind what we see as greed is always fear, and that makes it a lot harder to be judgmental. Practicing nonjudgment becomes very easy when you can see others with more compassion and understanding, and that starts with seeing yourself that way.

Gossip

One of the most self-destructive things we do is gossip. When we say negative things about others, all we're doing is sending out and attracting back to us ... yup, more negative energy. But there's even more to it.

If you feel the need to make others look worse by spreading gossip about them, it's an indication that you don't feel very good about yourself. People who truly feel comfortable with themselves just want others to feel good too.

By trying to make others the focus of negative attention, you are actually just trying to distract yourself—and others—from your own issues of insecurity.

Next time you want to gossip about someone, stop and ask yourself if you are just jealous of them. Maybe they are daring to do something that you feel not good enough to try. Instead of covering that insecurity with gossip, try offering them your admiration and see if it doesn't make you feel better.

This will then attract positive energy, experiences, and feelings to you—and who knows? It just may boost your confidence and help you let go of some of that self-doubt that's been holding you back.

FEAR

The cave you fear to enter holds the treasure you seek.
—Joseph Campbell

Everyone has fears. Some of us are more aware of our fears than others. Some have been through experiences that made them fearful. Some are afraid of real things, like getting robbed or hurt. Some are not sure what they're afraid of. A vague sense of fear just seems to always be there.

Some fears seem irrational, like claustrophobia or fear of heights. And some are shared with the society that you live in. These are the particularly tricky ones because when everyone around you is doing it, you can more easily believe that it's a healthy behavior. Most people consider buying life insurance or having a savings account to be a smart thing to do, but on a spiritual path, they mean that you do not trust life to take care of you. That does not make it wrong. But fear is an energy, like all emotions. And like attracts like.

In *A Course in Miracles*, we are taught that there are only two emotions behind every action we take: fear or love. Which one do you think motivates your "practical" choices? I have taught in my workshops for years the importance of looking within before making a decision. The rational mind is often blind to the fact that fear is running the show. Only by stepping out of it and observing oneself in meditation are we able to see whether it is fear or love that is motivating us. I have lived by one simple rule for a couple of decades now: If the motivator is fear, don't do it. If it's love, do it. Every time you choose love over fear, you weaken the hold that fear has on you.

This is the way to create the life that you desire. Only by freeing ourselves from our fears can we achieve this. Yes, everyone has fears, and most people you know allow their fears to guide their actions. Many people will argue that it's not that simple; that not taking certain precautions would be simply foolish. Meditation will help you to see that this thought is just part of your conditioning. You have a choice to make, and you will make it over and over again. Do you want to free yourself of the grip that fear has on you? Would you like to be able to leave that unhealthy relationship? Quit that treadmill job? Stand up to that controlling or manipulative person in your life?

How about moving to your dream destination? Opening that business you've been dreaming of for years or writing that book? Deep inside, you know the life that you are meant to be living. It may feel like a longing, a yearning, a dream. It's possible, but you will need to get past your fears to get there.

Is it possible to be completely fearless? Perhaps. Fear is an aspect of ego, and meditation frees us from ego, so it would follow that the more you meditate, the less afraid you are. If only that were true. Many spiritual teachers will agree that the further you go, the deeper you look into yourself, the more you release ego, the worse the fears become.

Buddhist nun and author Cheri Huber writes:

> It is true that as spiritual practice deepens, fear increases. Egocentricity, karmic conditioning, the illusion of a separate self, and suffering are one and the same, and the way they feel to us is what we call fear. When the control of conditioning is threatened, conditioning reacts with more fear. Sadly, we have learned to identify so strongly with conditioning that we assume it is ourselves who fear, and we go into defensive maneuvers that conditioning has learned to use to protect itself. ...
>
> Conditioning will pull out all the stops to get us back. Death, destruction, annihilation, the loss of all we hold dear. [However], you can learn to hold out.

It's entirely possible, and even likely, that you will have to face fear more often as you progress on your spiritual journey. You may find yourself dealing with fears you thought you had overcome, but now it is a deeper layer of those fears. Don't be discouraged.

If we make the choice to take some conscious breaths instead of turning to our usual coping behaviors when fear starts to surface, we gradually loosen the grip it has on us. Every time you give in to that compulsive drive to eat, drink, gamble, shop, play video games, or you fill in the blank, fear wins.

And every time you choose to sit with that horrible feeling that the world as you know it is about to fall apart; that something awful is going to happen to you or your loved ones; that you can barely breathe and your body feels like it is filled with tiny organisms that are crawling up and down inside your veins, you get stronger. As you sit with this feeling and focus on your breathing, you will see over and over that there was actually nothing to be afraid of. The thing you feared would happen didn't, and everyone, including you, is still fine.

Facing these feelings is not only liberating; it's a doorway to finding out even more about your conditioned self and the hidden beliefs that are running your life. Where are the fears coming from? A belief that you don't deserve to be this happy? A belief that if you don't stay in control (ego), something bad will happen? That it's your fault if something bad happens, as if you were God?

These beliefs are what give fear its power and hold on you. Use your meditation to uncover them and free yourself.

Exercise

Reflect for a moment on your childhood.

1. What kind of things were you afraid of? The dark? Dogs? Being alone? Getting spanked/punished/in trouble? Not having enough? Failing? Getting mugged? Death?
2. In what way did these fears influence/inhibit your behavior (e.g., I never spoke up because I was afraid I'd get in trouble)?
3. How many of these behaviors do you still see in yourself today?
4. Are you a practical person? What does that mean to you?
5. What would happen if you did something ridiculously impractical but fun? Is there someone who would be upset with you? Judge you?

Meditation

Relax your body and begin to focus on your breath. After a few minutes of observing your breath, have the intention to breathe in the energy of love and breathe out fear. With each breath, repeat, "I breathe in love … I breathe out fear," in your mind. Do this for as long as it takes for you to feel calmer. I usually find twenty to thirty minutes is enough. Don't try to force the fear out but instead just relax enough to allow it to gently be released; replaced by love. If you believe in a higher power, you could ask for the fear to be removed, by saying, "I'm aware of the fear inside me and I'm willing to release it now." Then just relax and breathe.

Worry

Most of us would not think that by worrying we are blocking ourselves from abundance, but that is, in fact, the case. Worry is connected to fear, which is one of the lowest vibrations of emotional energy. When we allow ourselves to get caught up in our worries about the future, the safety of a loved one, our finances, health, and so on, what we are really doing is sending out the energy and vision that will attract the very thing we fear into our lives! Think of it. If you worry about getting sick because someone on the bus sneezed beside you, you will often imagine what it will feel like, in what way it will interfere with your plans, how long it will take for you to feel better, how miserable you felt last time … You're basically sending your worry as a visualization into the Universe!

We often do this to our children. We see them climbing up on a chair to reach something in the cupboard. "Be careful! You're going to fall!" we might say, not realizing that we are planting that idea in their heads as well as cocreating it with our own energy. Then, when it happens, we say, "I told you so!"

This is so unfair to our children because we are the ones who made them fall through our worry, and then we blame it on them.

My Story

I was in Germany, visiting with a good friend. Kurt was back home in France. I had driven over in our car—his car really but the only one we had. (He'd promised to get me my own car if I came with him to France, but once we got there, he made excuses not to.) My friend Eva-Maria was twelve years older than me and a deep thinker. We always had great talks together— exploring and learning about life, love, and the whole crazy mess of human relationships. Since I'd been living in France, I really missed these visits.

As we walked back to where I'd parked, I noticed a ticket on the windshield. *Oh no! I overstayed the time on my meter!* I was immediately filled with dread and panic. How could I hide this from Kurt? He would be very angry with me for this—in his eyes—carelessness. He would certainly never have allowed it to happen if he'd been there. He'd have kept an eye on his watch. How could I have been so irresponsible—throwing money out the window like that?

Before meeting him, I would never have been so upset about something as small as a parking ticket, but here I was, reduced to a frightened child. Since moving to France, we only had one joint bank account, so there would be no way of hiding this from Kurt.

Eva-Maria watched me with concern. After the talk we'd had, it was like I'd turned into another person. Where was my confidence? Why was this such a big deal? She didn't say anything, but I could see in her face that she was noticing this sudden shift in my energy.

Not really expecting an answer, I asked her, "Why does this make me so scared? What am I afraid of?"

It was a big step that I was even asking that question. I had been that way for so long, I wouldn't have even noticed anything was wrong with reacting that way.

Eva looked at me with compassion as she touched my arm. "It's love," she said. "You're afraid of losing his love."

I will never forget that moment. With that profound insight disguised as the simplest of statements, Eva changed my life. What else was I doing to avoid the feeling of being unloved, and where had this started in the first place? The quest began to find out why I had given Kurt this kind of power over me.

I realized that I never got the unconditional love that I deserved in my family, so there was nothing to fall back on there. I soon found a book by Louise Hay that helped me to see that I could give myself that love, and combining that knowledge with my meditation practice got me there. It took a few years, but I could feel gradual improvement every day. In the end, I not only learned to love myself, but I was blessed many times with experiencing the presence of divine love in my meditations.

When you know that you are loved, other people have no more power over you. When you know that you are loved, there is nothing to fear. If someone is disappointed with me for something today, I know that that is their issue, and it doesn't shake me for more than a few seconds.

In my life, love now sits where fear used to—in the driver's seat. Fear keeps trying to crawl forward and take over again, but meditation puts it back where it belongs every time.

Final Thoughts

It took me a few years to write this book. The process of sharing my story turned out to be a deeply healing experience. As I look back at all I went through, I now understand fully that it was all my own projection. I didn't know anything other than what I'd learned in my childhood, so I kept repeating those patterns until I learned to look within. Yes, I have a healthy relationship with a loving partner today. That is my external reality. But more importantly, I have a healthy relationship with myself.

The fact that I've attracted Jon into my life today is proof that I now truly love and respect myself. He is a reflection of that. And as much as I saw Kurt as the problem, the source of my suffering, the threat to my safety, the truth as I see it today is that he too was merely a reflection of the way I saw myself at the time.

The Universe will show us what we can't see in ourselves by making it show up in someone else. It's sad to see that I was so self-rejecting, self-judging, self-denying that I had to sink so low before I finally found the strength and courage to stand up for myself. I had to hit rock bottom. Kurt was my teacher and, ACIM would even say, my savior. If he hadn't come along and played the role that he did in my life, I might never have embarked on this journey of remembering who I truly am.

"You are my beloved child, in whom I am well pleased." I remember hearing these words in a meditation once and being filled with joy, love, and relief that God was so pleased with me. I felt pleased, too, with who I was becoming. It's been a long journey, and I know better than to believe it's over. But the worst is behind me. I don't know what lies ahead, but I know that along my journey, I've gathered tools, gained strength, and built faith enough to know that I'll make it through.

When I was going through the scariest, toughest, loneliest part of my divorce back in Germany years ago, my sister sent me an email with this message: *If God brought you to it, He'll see you through it.*

I printed it out and hung it on my bedroom door. I read it every day. I breathed it in and let it sink into my cells. I trusted that thought, and it turned out to be true.

Our toughest times can be our greatest opportunities for growth, if we let them.

Our most vicious enemies can be our greatest teachers.

Our biggest challenges can turn out to be the greatest miracles in our lives, if we open our hearts and minds to let Spirit walk with us through them.

If we don't get this, we are missing the whole point of why we are here. Life is a classroom, but the Teacher is not going to force you to do your work. Only your internal guidance can tell you if you are doing what you are supposed to here. It will be messy, challenging, terrifying, rewarding, amazing, peaceful, confusing, and miraculous. But all along the way, it will feel meaningful. Even when your mind questions if you're on the right path, the still, small voice in your heart will reassure you that you are if you ask it. Take a deep breath and trust that voice.

Printed in the United States
by Baker & Taylor Publisher Services

Printed in the United States
by Baker & Taylor Publisher Services